LUXURY WINERY ESTATES

edited by Christian Datz and Christof Kullmann

teNeues

Burgundy

Bordeaux

Burgenland

Aragon

Rioja
Navarra

Rheingau

South Tyrol

Palatinate

Toscana

Württemberg

Piedmont

California

Cape Winelands

Luxury Winery Estates

The refined world of excellent wines

This book takes you into the world of exclusive winery estates: Discover majestic architecture, some of which is centuries old, surrounded by lush gardens and vast vineyards as well as modern, extravagant buildings that give a contemporary voice to the self-confidence of internationally renowned estates. Discover how function and representation merge into splendid estates and use of space—as evidenced by both mighty cellar vaults and impressive production sites, as well as by the stylish, often luxurious living space of the estate owners. Just like a wine is characterized by its acreage, soil and climate, the diverse architecture of the winery estates mirror the characteristics of the vineyards, which are unique to each region. Here the character and forms of the landscape also play a vital role, as does the political, cultural and economic history of the various regions.

Our journey through the famous wine-growing regions of the world starts in California, or in Napa Valley, to be more precise. This growing region has a comparably recent history—cultivation didn't start here on a large scale until the 19th Century. Optimal geological, geographic and climatic conditions in connection with modern cultivation and production methods have helped Napa Valley take up a leading position worldwide since at least the 1960s. The new structures of the more recent winery estates bear witness to the independent way wine culture from this region has taken. Spain, a classic wine-growing nation, also boasts a multitude of wineries today that are as innovative as they are exclusive: Take, for example, the highly traditional Marqués de Riscal winery, which commissioned star architect Frank O. Gehry to build a spectacular wine hotel right next to its historic buildings. On the other hand, estates such as Señorío de Otazu and Señorío de Arínzano rely on more subtle ways of blending old with new. One of the most striking examples of more recent winery architecture was created by architect Santiago Calatrava with the Bodegas Ysios for the large winery Domecq Bodegas.

In contrast, the famous French vineyards of Bordeaux and Burgundy are all about tradition. Here the estates lie as magnificent castles in the middle of vast vineyards, powerfully underscoring the wealth and self-confidence of their builders. The fact that these winery estates are ultimately agricultural businesses too stays completely on the sidelines in view of their noble façades. The origin of the French winery estates can quite often be traced back to the 13th and 14th Centuries, although most of them have changed owners over the course of the centuries. In recent times, a whole row of traditional estates has been purchased by celebrity athletes or wealthy business people. However, they weren't just motivated by profit and prestige; rather they have dedicated their passion and heavy financial commitment to the production of superb wines. Wine growing in Germany is deeply rooted in tradition as well, as evidenced by examples in this book. Wineries such as Robert Weil, Dr. Bürklin-Wolf and Fürst zu Hohenlohe-Oehringen present themselves with pride in their historic estates. In contrast, there is the current, much discussed "wine wonder" in Austria, represented here by the ultramodern new design of the Leo Hillinger winery.

Particularly vivid are without a doubt the diverse, changing relationships between the land, history, architecture and wine cultivation in the famous wine regions of Tuscany. Defiant castellos—once erected as forts in this region that has been shaped by centuries of war chaos and power struggles—were later converted into winery estates. Some of these estates, such as the Castello di Fonterutoli or Barone Ricasoli, have been family-owned for centuries: A remarkable continuity, which is also reflected in the richly decorated, gorgeous interiors of these estates. However, the vineyards to the north, such as southern Tyrol or the Piedmont, also have their share of wines and wine estates with their own unique characters, which are as famous as they are exquisite. The end of our journey takes us to South Africa, which can also look back on a long history of wine cultivation. In fact, in the middle of the 17th Century Jan van Riebeeck, the founder of the Cape Colony, brought the first vines into the country and planted them at the foot of Table Mountain. French Huguenots and German wine growers then laid the foundation for today's structure and quality of South African wine cultivation. However, the far-reaching political and economic isolation of the country as a result of apartheid led to the fact that South African wines have only gained international awareness and recognition within the last twenty years.

Today, wine is an everyday indulgence for many people across the globe—every supermarket sells inexpensive products from all over the world. *Luxury Winery Estates* presents the other end of the scale: A selection of excellent top wineries, whose buildings and interiors reflect the sophistication, quality and success of wine culture at its best.

Christian Datz, Christof Kullmann

Die noble Welt der exzellenten Weine

Dieses Buch entführt den Leser in die Welt exklusiver Weingüter: Herrschaftliche, zum Teil jahrhundertealte Architekturen, umgeben von üppigen Gärten und ausgedehnten Weinbergen finden sich hier ebenso wie moderne, extravagante Gebäude, die dem Selbstbewusstsein international renommierter Güter einen zeitgemäßen Ausdruck verleihen. Funktionalität und Repräsentation verbinden sich hier zu großartigen Anwesen und Raumschöpfungen – dies zeigt sich sowohl in mächtigen Kellergewölben und beeindruckenden Produktionsanlagen, als auch in den stilvollen, oftmals luxuriösen Wohnräumen der Gutsbesitzer. So wie der Wein durch die Lage, den Boden und das Klima geprägt ist, spiegeln sich auch in den unterschiedlichen Architekturen der Weingüter die regional typischen Besonderheiten der Anbaugebiete. Auch hierbei spielen Charakter und Formen der Landschaft eine große Rolle, ebenso wie die politische, kulturelle und wirtschaftliche Geschichte der verschiedenen Regionen.

Die Reise durch die berühmten Weinbaugebiete der Welt beginnt in Kalifornien, genauer gesagt im Napa Valley. Diese Anbauregion hat eine vergleichsweise junge Geschichte – erst seit dem 19. Jahrhundert wird hier in größerem Umfang Wein angebaut. Optimale geologische, geographische und klimatische Bedingungen in Verbindung mit modernen Anbau- und Produktionsmethoden haben dazu geführt, dass das Napa Valley spätestens seit den 60er-Jahren des vergangenen Jahrhunderts weltweit eine Spitzenposition einnimmt. Die neuen Bauten der jüngeren Weingüter belegen, wie eigenständig sich die Weinkultur dieser Region entwickelt hat. Auch in Spanien, einer klassischen Weinbaunation, findet sich heute eine Vielzahl ebenso innovativer wie exklusiver Gutsanlagen: So ließ das traditionsreiche Weingut Marqués de Riscal durch den Stararchitekten Frank O. Gehry direkt neben seine historischen Gebäude ein spektakuläres Weinhotel errichten. Güter wie Señorío de Otazu und Señorío de Arínzano hingegen setzten auf subtilere Verbindungen von Alt und Neu. Eines der markantesten Beispiele neuerer Weingutsarchitektur schuf der Architekt Santiago Calatrava mit der Bodegas Ysios für die Großkellerei Domecq Bodegas.

Ganz im Zeichen der Tradition hingegen stehen die berühmten französischen Anbaugebiete Bordeaux und Burgund. Als herrschaftliche Schlösser liegen hier die Güter inmitten ausgedehnter Weinberge und unterstreichen eindrucksvoll den Reichtum und das Selbstbewusstsein ihrer Erbauer. Dass auch diese Weingüter letztlich landwirtschaftliche Betriebe sind, tritt angesichts ihrer noblen Fassaden völlig in den Hintergrund. Der Ursprung der französischen Weingüter lässt sich nicht selten bis in das 13. und 14. Jahrhundert zurückverfolgen; meist kam es jedoch im Laufe der Jahrhunderte mehrfach zu Besitzerwechseln. In jüngerer Vergangenheit wurde eine ganze Reihe von Traditionsgütern von prominenten Sportlern oder wohlhabenden Geschäftsleuten gekauft, die dabei jedoch nicht nur Rendite und Prestige im Sinne hatten, sondern sich mit Leidenschaft und großem finanziellen Engagement der Produktion von Spitzenweinen verschrieben haben. Auch in Deutschland ist der Weinbau tief in der Tradition verwurzelt, wie die Beispiele in diesem Buch belegen. Güter wie Robert Weil, Dr. Bürklin-Wolf und Fürst zu Hohenlohe-Oehringen präsentieren sich stolz in ihren historischen Höfen. Demgegenüber steht das aktuelle, vieldiskutierte „Weinwunder" in Österreich, das hier mit dem ultramodernen Neubau des Weingutes Leo Hillinger repräsentiert ist.

Besonders anschaulich sind die vielfältigen Wechselbeziehungen von Landschaft, Geschichte, Architektur und Weinbau zweifellos in den berühmten Anbauregionen der Toskana. Trutzige Castellos – einst als Festungsanlagen in der über Jahrhunderte von Kriegswirren und Machtkämpfen bestimmten Region errichtet – wurden später in Weingüter umgewandelt. Einige dieser Güter – wie beispielsweise das Castello di Fonterutoli oder Barone Ricasoli – sind schon seit Jahrhunderten in Familienbesitz: Eine beeindruckende Kontinuität, die sich auch an den reich dekorierten, prunkvollen Innenräumen ablesen lässt. Doch auch in den nördlicheren Anbaugebieten wie Südtirol oder dem Piemont finden sich ebenso berühmte wie exquisite Weine und Weingüter mit ganz besonderem Charakter. Am Ende der Reise steht Südafrika, das ebenfalls auf eine lange Weinbaugeschichte zurückblickt. Schon Jan van Riebeeck, der Gründer der Kapkolonie, hatte Mitte des 17. Jahrhunderts die ersten Reben ins Land gebracht und am Fuße des Tafelberges gepflanzt. Französische Hugenotten und deutsche Weinbauern legten in der Folge den Grundstein für die heutige Struktur und Qualität des südafrikanischen Weinbaus. Die weitgehende politische und wirtschaftliche Isolierung des Landes als Folge der Apartheid führte allerdings dazu, dass die südafrikanischen Weine erst in den letzten zwanzig Jahren internationale Beachtung und Anerkennung erfahren konnten.

Wein ist heute für viele Menschen auf der ganzen Welt ein alltäglicher Genuss – längst findet man in jedem Supermarkt preiswerte Angebote aus aller Welt. *Luxury Winery Estates* präsentiert das andere Ende des Spektrums: Eine Auswahl exzellenter Spitzenweingüter, in deren Gebäuden und Innenräumen sich Anspruch, Qualität und Erfolg höchster Weinkultur widerspiegeln.

Christian Datz, Christof Kullmann

L'univers fastueux des vins d'excellence

Ce livre entraîne le lecteur dans le monde des domaines viticoles exclusifs : des architectures seigneuriales, pour certaines, vieilles de plusieurs siècles, entourées de jardins luxuriants et de vignobles étendus, côtoient des bâtiments modernes et extravagants ; ceux-ci sont l'expression moderne de la réussite de ces domaines de renommée internationale. C'est ici que sont conjugués fonctionnalité et art de la représentation, aboutissant à la création de propriétés magnifiques et d'espaces innovants – ceci se retrouve dans des caves aux voûtes imposantes et des installations de production impressionnantes mais aussi dans les demeures de bon goût, souvent luxueuses, des propriétaires. De même que l'exposition, le terroir et le climat confèrent son caractère au vin, de même les particularités locales des régions de production se reflètent dans les différentes architectures des domaines. Ici aussi, le caractère et les formes du paysage jouent un grand rôle, tout comme l'histoire politique, culturelle et économique des diverses régions.

Le voyage autour du monde des vignobles célèbres commence en Californie, précisément dans la vallée de Napa. Cette région viticole a une histoire relativement récente – ce n'est qu'à partir du 19ème siècle que la vigne y fut cultivée à grande échelle. Grâce à des conditions géologiques, géographiques et climatiques optimales, associées à des méthodes de culture et de production modernes, la vallée de Napa se plaça au premier plan dans le monde dès les années soixante du siècle dernier. Les constructions neuves des domaines plus récents prouvent que la culture du vin dans cette région s'est développée de façon autonome. En Espagne également, nation de tradition viticole, on trouve de nos jours une multitude de propriétés aussi innovatrices qu'exclusives : c'est ainsi que le domaine viticole, riche en traditions, Marqués de Riscal, fit construire par la star de l'architecture, Frank O. Gehry, un hôtel spectaculaire à la gloire du vin, directement à côté de ses bâtiments historiques. En revanche, des domaines comme Señorío de Otazu et Señorío de Arínzano misèrent sur des associations plus subtiles d'ancien et de moderne. L'un des exemples les plus frappants du renouveau de l'architecture des domaines viticoles est la Bodega d'Ysios, créée par l'architecte Santiago Calatrava, pour les grandes Bodegas Domecq.

Par contre, les célèbres vignobles français du Bordelais et de Bourgogne restent placés sous le signe de la tradition. Les domaines seigneuriaux trônent au cœur de vignes étendues et soulignent de façon impressionnante la richesse et l'assurance de leurs fondateurs. Le fait que ces domaines restent finalement des entreprises agricoles passe complètement inaperçu, tant leurs façades sont nobles. L'origine des domaines français remonte souvent aux 13ème et 14ème siècles ; au fil des siècles, cependant, les propriétaires ont souvent changé. Ces derniers temps, une série de domaines de grande tradition fut achetée par des sportifs éminents ou des hommes d'affaires fortunés, qui ne pensaient pas seulement au rendement et au prestige mais qui se sont voués, passionnément et avec d'importants apports financiers, à la production de vins haut de gamme. En Allemagne aussi, la viticulture est profondément ancrée dans les traditions ; les exemples dans ce livre en témoignent. Dans leurs cours historiques, les domaines Robert Weil, Dr. Bürklin-Wolf et Fürst zu Hohenlohe-Oehringen s'affichent fièrement. A l'opposé, on rencontre en Autriche l'actuel « miracle œnologique », très controversé et représenté par le bâtiment neuf ultramoderne du domaine Leo Hillinger.

Sans conteste, les multiples aspects de l'interdépendance du paysage, de l'histoire, de l'architecture et de la viticulture sont particulièrement évidents dans les célèbres régions de production de la Toscane. Des « castellos » bien défendus – construits jadis comme fortifications dans cette région soumise pendant des siècles aux troubles des guerres et aux luttes de pouvoir – furent plus tard transformés en domaines viticoles. Certains de ces domaines – comme par exemple le Castello di Fonterutoli ou Barone Ricasoli – sont depuis des siècles des propriétés familiales : une continuité impressionnante, qu'illustrent bien leurs intérieurs somptueux, richement décorés. Pourtant, les régions du nord, comme le Tyrol du Sud ou le Piémont, offrent des vins aussi réputés qu'excellents et des domaines viticoles de caractère. Le voyage s'achève en Afrique du Sud où la viticulture a également une longue histoire. Jan van Riebeeck, le fondateur de la Colonie du Cap, avait apporté les premiers sarments de vigne dans le pays dès le milieu du 17ème siècle et les avait plantés au pied du Table Mountain. Par la suite, des huguenots français et des vignerons allemands furent les précurseurs de la structure et de la qualité de la viticulture sud-africaine. Le grand isolement politique et économique du pays, dû à la politique de l'apartheid, ne permit aux vins sud-africains de conquérir le respect et la reconnaissance internationale qu'au cours de ces vingt dernières années.

Aujourd'hui, le vin représente un plaisir quotidien pour des millions d'hommes de par le monde – on trouve depuis longtemps dans chaque supermarché des produits peu coûteux venant du monde entier. *Luxury Winery Estates* vous en présente la genèse : une sélection de domaines prestigieux dont les bâtiments et les intérieurs reflètent l'exigence, la qualité et la réussite d'une culture du vin de grande classe.

Christian Datz, Christof Kullmann

El exquisito mundo de los vinos selectos

Esta obra seduce al lector trasladándolo a un mundo de bodegas exclusivas. Arquitecturas señoriales, algunas de ellas centenarias, enmarcadas con exuberantes jardines y vastos viñedos, frente a extravagantes y modernos edificios, que aportan un carácter contemporáneo a renombradas bodegas internacionales. Aquí la funcionalidad y la imagen se funden convirtiéndose en impresionantes dominios y creaciones de espacios, como muestran las imponentes bodegas abovedadas y edificios de producción, o las elegantes, muchas además lujosas, viviendas de sus propietarios. Del mismo modo que en el vino influyen la ubicación, el suelo y el clima, en las diferentes arquitecturas se reflejan las particularidades regionales típicas de las zonas vitícolas. Todo juega un papel importante: tanto el carácter y las formas del paisaje como la historia política y cultural de las regiones.

Nuestro viaje por las famosas zonas vitivinícolas del mundo comienza en California, concretamente en el Valle de Napa. Esta región de cultivo cuenta con una historia relativamente reciente, puesto que aquí no se comenzó a cultivar vid a gran escala hasta el siglo XIX. Las óptimas condiciones geológicas, geográficas y climáticas unidas a modernos métodos de cultivo y producción han logrado que, prácticamente desde los años 60 del siglo pasado, el Valle de Napa se encuentre a la cabeza a nivel mundial. Las nuevas construcciones de bodegas más recientes muestran la independencia con la que se ha desarrollado la cultura del vino en esta región. También en España, nación vitivinícola por excelencia, existen hoy numerosas bodegas igual de innovadoras y exclusivas. Ejemplo de ello es la tradicional Marqués de Riscal, en la que el famoso arquitecto Frank O. Gehry ha concebido un espectacular hotel del vino junto al edificio histórico. Mientras tanto, dominios como el Señorío de Arínzano han optado por la sutil fusión entre lo antiguo y lo moderno. Uno de los más destacados ejemplos de arquitectura moderna de bodegas es la obra del arquitecto Santiago Calatrava con sus Bodegas Ysios, pertenecientes a la gran casa Domecq.

Las célebres zonas vitivinícolas de Burdeos y Borgoña permanecen en cambio arraigadas a la tradición. En ellas se levantan castillos señoriales en medio de dominios dibujados por vastos viñedos que acentúan la imponente riqueza y el orgullo de sus fundadores. Ante semejantes nobles fachadas, lo que en definitiva no deja de ser una empresa agrícola queda relegado a un segundo plano. El origen de no pocos de los dominios vitícolas franceses se remonta a los siglos XIII y XIV, y muchos de ellos han cambiado de propietario en diversas ocasiones a lo largo de los siglos. En un pasado más reciente han sido deportistas famosos e influyentes personalidades del mundo de los negocios quienes han comprado propiedades con tradición, si bien no sólo con el objeto de obtener beneficios y prestigio, sino entregándose con pasión y esfuerzo financiero a la producción de vinos de élite. En Alemania el cultivo vitivinícola tiene igualmente una tradición arraigada, documentada en los ejemplos de este libro. Propiedades como las de Robert Weil, Dr. Bürklin-Wolf y el Fürst zu Hohenlohe-Oehringen se presentan orgullosas y envueltas en un halo histórico. Frente a ellas aparece el actual y tan discutido "milagro vitícola" de Austria, que la obra muestra a través de la ultramoderna construcción de las bodegas Leo Hillinger.

Los vínculos cambiantes entre paisaje, historia, arquitectura y cultivo de la vid en las famosas zonas de producción de la Toscana son sin duda significativos. Robustos castellos, en su día fortalezas que durante siglos fueron testigo de los avatares de las guerras y luchas por el poder, se transformaron más tarde en bodegas. Algunas de estas propiedades, como es el caso del Castello di Fonterutoli o del Barone Ricasoli, son patrimonio de la familia desde hace siglos; con ello se ha forjado una continuidad que se percibe en las ricas y suntuosas decoraciones de sus interiores. Pero también en zonas de cultivo situadas más al norte, como Tirol del Sur y Piamonte, se encuentran vinos exquisitos y bodegas de extraordinario carácter. El viaje concluye en Sudáfrica, que cuenta igualmente con una larga historia en la producción de vino. Ya a mediados del siglo XVII Jan van Riebeeck, el fundador de la colonia de El Cabo, introdujo en el país las primeras cepas para plantarlas a los pies de la cordillera de Table Mountain. Hugonotes franceses y viticultores alemanes continuaron sentando las bases de la estructura y calidad de la que goza hoy la producción de vino sudafricana. El prolongado aislamiento político y económico, como resultado del apartheid, ha sido sin embargo la consecuencia de que los vinos sudafricanos no hayan recibido el debido reconocimiento internacional hasta los últimos veinte años.

El vino es hoy en todo el planeta un placer diario; y ya hace tiempo que los supermercados disponen de una interesante oferta de vinos procedentes del mundo entero. *Luxury Winery Estates* propone, sin embargo, una visión al otro extremo: una selección de excelentes bodegas de élite cuyos edificios e interiores reflejan la exigencia, la calidad y el éxito de la cultura del vino más exquisita.

Christian Datz, Christof Kullmann

Lo squisito mondo dei vini di gran classe

Questo libro rapisce il lettore nel mondo delle più esclusive tenute vinicole: un mondo che vede architetture signorili dalla storia in parte plurisecolare, circondate da giardini lussureggianti ed ampi vigneti, accanto a edifici moderni e stravaganti, creati per esprimere in un linguaggio moderno l'orgoglio di aziende vinicole rinomate a livello internazionale. Qui aspetti funzionali e volontà di rappresentazione si fondono per realizzare grandiose tenute e creazioni architettoniche: ne danno prova evidente tanto cantine dal possente soffitto a volte e imponenti impianti di vinificazione, quanto anche le abitazioni eleganti e spesso lussuose dei proprietari delle aziende stesse. Come il vino è il prodotto di un certo vigneto, terreno e clima, così nelle differenti architetture delle tenute si rispecchiano le peculiarità regionali tipiche delle varie aree a vocazione vitivinicola. Anche qui svolgono un ruolo fondamentale il carattere e le forme del paesaggio, come pure la storia politica, culturale e economica delle singole regioni.

Il viaggio attraverso le più note aree di produzione vinicola del mondo ha inizio in California, per la precisione nella Napa Valley. Questa regione vinicola ha una storia relativamente breve, infatti vi si coltiva la vite in grande scala solo dall'Ottocento. Ideali condizioni geologiche, geografiche e climatiche, unitamente a moderni metodi di coltivazione e produzione, hanno fatto sì che la Napa Valley, al più tardi a partire dagli anni Sessanta dello scorso secolo, occupasse una posizione di punta a livello mondiale. I nuovi edifici delle tenute di più recente costruzione dimostrano con quanta autonomia si sia andata sviluppando la cultura vinicola di questa regione. Anche in Spagna, una classica nazione a vocazione vinicola, oggi è facile imbattersi in un gran numero di tenute vinicole che abbinano esclusività e innovazione. Così, per esempio, la tradizionale tenuta vinicola Marqués de Riscal ha fatto erigere dal rinomato architetto Frank O. Gehry un "hotel del vino", nelle immediate vicinanze dei suoi edifici storici. Altri invece, come per esempio le tenute Señorío de Otazu e Señorío de Arínzano, hanno puntato su più sottili commissioni di vecchio e nuovo. Uno degli esempi più incisivi della recente architettura enologica è senz'altro il progetto realizzato per il gigante Domecq Bodegas dall'architetto Santiago Calatrava con le Bodegas Ysios.

Una grande fedeltà alla tradizione, invece, caratterizza le celebri regioni vinicole del Bordeaux e della Borgogna: qui le tenute, dominate da signorili castelli, si trovano al centro di vigneti a perdita d'occhio e sottolineano con forza la ricchezza e l'orgoglio dei loro costruttori. In effetti, a guardare le nobili facciate, quasi si dimentica che in fin dei conti anche queste tenute sono delle aziende agricole. L'origine dei poderi vinicoli francesi non di rado risale sino al XIII e XIV secolo, anche se per lo più nel corso dei secoli si sono verificati numerosi cambi di proprietà. Nel passato più recente tutta una serie di poderi di antica tradizione è stata acquistata da sportivi di successo o da agiati uomini d'affari, che però non puntavano solo a ricavarne reddito e prestigio, bensì si sono dedicati con passione e grande impegno finanziario alla produzione di vini di altissima qualità. Anche in Germania la coltivazione della vite è fortemente radicata nella tradizione, come testimoniano gli esempi citati in questo libro. Tenute come Robert Weil, Dr. Bürklin-Wolf e Fürst zu Hohenlohe-Oehringen si presentano in tutta la fierezza delle loro dimore storiche. Fa loro da contrappeso l'attualissimo, assai discusso "miracolo vinicolo" austriaco, qui rappresentato dall'ultramoderno edificio di nuova costruzione della tenuta Leo Hillinger.

Senza dubbio v'è un luogo in cui le molteplici correlazioni tra paesaggio, storia, architettura e vinicoltura sono particolarmente evidenti: nelle rinomate regioni viti-vinicole della Toscana. Castelli fortificati, originariamente costruiti a scopo difensivo in una regione che per secoli fu scenario di guerre e lotte di potere, sono stati successivamente trasformati in tenute vinicole. Alcune di queste, come per esempio il Castello di Fonterutoli o quello del Barone Ricasoli, sono proprietà della stessa famiglia ormai da secoli: una continuità che lascia ammirati e di cui si possono riconoscere i segni evidenti anche nei sontuosi interni riccamente decorati. Ma anche nelle regioni vinicole più settentrionali, come l'Alto Adige o il Piemonte, si trovano vini tanto famosi quanto squisiti e tenute vinicole dal carattere inconfondibile. Al termine del nostro viaggio ecco il Sudafrica, che pure ha alle spalle una lunga storia vitivinicola: già Jan van Riebeeck, il fondatore della colonia del Capo, verso la metà del XVII secolo aveva portato nella regione i primi vitigni e li aveva fatti impiantare ai piedi del Table Mountain. Successivamente ugonotti francesi e viticoltori tedeschi gettarono le fondamenta per l'attuale struttura e qualità della vinicoltura sudafricana. Il grave isolamento politico ed economico in cui il Paese si venne a trovare a causa dell'apartheid, tuttavia, ha permesso solo negli ultimi vent'anni ai vini sudafricani di riscuotere attenzione e riconoscimento a livello internazionale.

Per molti oggi il vino è, in tutto il mondo, un piacere quotidiano: in ogni supermercato ormai è possibile trovare vini a buon mercato di ogni provenienza. *Luxury Winery Estates* presenta l'altra faccia della medaglia: una selezione di eccellenti tenute vinicole di spicco, nei cui edifici e nei cui interni si rispecchiano le ambizioni, la qualità ed il successo della più raffinata cultura enologica.

Christian Datz, Christof Kullmann

Opus One
California, USA

Opus One was founded in the late 1970s in Napa Valley as a joint project of the California-based Robert Mondavi winery and Château Mouton-Rothschild of France—the idea was to produce an exquisite Californian wine with the characteristics of a Bordeaux. Indeed, the wine bearing the same name today is one of the most highly rated and most expensive wines of America. Commissioned in 1991, the cellar with its complex design is situated amidst vast vine areas, giving voice to the claim and the success of the enterprise.

Opus One wurde Ende der 70er-Jahre im Napa Valley als Gemeinschaftsprojekt des kalifornischen Weingutes Robert Mondavi und dem französischen Château Mouton-Rothschild gegründet – Ziel war die Produktion eines kalifornischen Spitzenweines mit den Charakteristika eines Bordeaux. Tatsächlich ist der gleichnamige Wein heute einer der am höchsten bewerteten und teuersten Weine der USA. Das 1991 in Betrieb genommene, aufwendig gestaltete Kellereigebäude liegt inmitten ausgedehnter Rebflächen und verleiht dem Anspruch und dem Erfolg des Unternehmens Ausdruck.

Opus One, créé à la fin des années 70 dans la vallée de Napa, est l'aboutissement d'un projet associant le domaine californien Robert Mondavi et le français Château Mouton-Rothschild – l'objectif était de produire un vin californien haut de gamme possédant les caractéristiques d'un Bordeaux. Et, en effet, le vin du même nom est aujourd'hui l'un des vins les plus cotés et les plus chers des Etats-Unis. Le bâtiment abritant les caves, une coûteuse réalisation mise en service en 1991, se dresse au milieu de vignes étendues et incarne l'exigence et la réussite de l'entreprise.

Opus One fue fundado a finales de los años 70 en el Valle de Napa, como proyecto en común entre la bodega californiana de Robert Mondavi y la francesa Château Mouton-Rothschild. El objetivo era la producción de un vino californiano de élite que estuviera dotado de las características del Burdeos. Y en efecto, el vino del mismo nombre es hoy uno de los mejor calificados y más caros de Estados Unidos. Los lujosamente equipados edificios de las bodegas, puestos en funcionamiento en 1991, están ubicados en medio de los vastos viñedos y caracterizan claramente el éxito y nivel de exigencia de la empresa.

Opus One è stata fondata nella Napa Valley sul finire degli anni Settanta nell'ambito di un progetto comune di due aziende vinicole, la californiana Robert Mondavi e la francese Château Mouton-Rothschild. L'obiettivo era produrre un vino californiano di gran classe che avesse le caratteristiche tipiche di un Bordeaux: in effetti oggi l'omonimo vino è in cima alle classifiche e tra i più cari di tutti gli Stati Uniti. L'edificio che ospita le cantine, entrato in funzione nel 1991 e allestito con notevole dispendio di mezzi, si trova al centro di estese coltivazioni a vite e rappresenta il simbolo visibile dell'ambizione e del successo dell'azienda.

Robert Mondavi and Baron Philippe de Rothschild, founders of Opus One

Robert Mondavi und Baron Philippe de Rothschild, Gründer von Opus One

Robert Mondavi et le baron Philippe de Rothschild, fondateurs d'Opus One

Robert Mondavi y Baron Philippe de Rothschild, fundadores de Opus One

Robert Mondavi e Baron Philippe de Rothschild, fondatori di Opus One

Johnson Fain Architects have created an unusual blend of modern and traditional designs, whose elements link the Old World with the New World.

Die Architekten Johnson Fain *schufen eine ungewöhnliche Mischung aus modernen und traditionellen Bauformen, deren Elemente Alte Welt und Neue Welt miteinander verbinden.*

Les architectes Johnson Fain *ont créé un mélange inhabituel de formes architecturales modernes et traditionnelles dont les éléments relient l'Ancien monde et le Nouveau monde.*

Los arquitectos de Johnson Fain *concibieron una peculiar fusión entre las formas de construcción modernas y tradicionales, cuyos elementos vinculan el Viejo y el Nuevo Mundo.*

Gli architetti della Johnson Fain *hanno realizzato un'insolita mescolanza di forme architettoniche moderne e tradizionali, i cui elementi collegano il Vecchio al Nuovo Mondo.*

Quintessa

California, USA

In 1989, wine merchant Agustin Huneeus and his wife Valeria came across one of the last areas in Napa Valley not yet developed for wine cultivation. They managed to purchase the property measuring at least 280 acres and to establish a new winery here: Quintessa. The name refers to five prominent hills located within the vineyards and to the aspiration of producing "quintessential" wines. The subterranean cellar, completed in 2002, is demarcated by a prominent, sickle-shaped, natural stone wall and harmoniously blends into the surrounding landscape.

Im Jahr 1989 stießen der Weinhändler Agustin Huneeus und seine Frau Valeria auf eine der letzten noch nicht für den Weinbau entwickelten Lagen im Napa Valley. Es gelang ihnen, den gut 113 ha umfassenden Besitz zu erwerben und hier ein neues Weingut zu gründen: Quintessa. Der Name bezieht sich auf fünf markante Hügel, die innerhalb der Anbauflächen zu finden sind, und auf den Anspruch, „quintessenzielle" Weine zu produzieren. Das unterirdische, 2002 fertiggestellte Kellereigebäude wird von einer markanten, sichelförmigen Natursteinmauer begrenzt und fügt sich harmonisch in die umgebende Landschaft ein.

En 1989, le négociant en vins Agustin Huneeus et sa femme Valeria découvrirent l'un des derniers sites de la vallée de Napa qui n'était pas encore aménagé pour la viti-culture. Ils réussirent à acquérir cette propriété d'au moins 113 hectares et à y fonder un nouveau domaine : Quintessa. Ce nom fait référence aux cinq coteaux, situés au cœur des vignes, et à l'exigence du domaine : produire des vins « quintessenciés ». Le bâtiment, achevé en 2002, abritant une cave souterraine, est délimité par un remarquable mur de pierre naturelle, en forme de faucille, et se fond harmonieusement dans le paysage environnant.

En el año 1989 el comerciante de vinos Agustin Huneeus y su mujer Valeria toparon con una de las últimas zonas aún por explotar del Valle de Napa. Consiguieron adquirir una finca de 113 hectáreas y fundaron en ella las bodegas Quintessa. El nombre se refiere a las cinco características colinas que se levantan sobre el terreno, así como a las exigencias de producir vinos "de la quintaesencia". El edificio bodega subterráneo concluido en 2002 está circundado por un muro de piedra destacado en forma de hoz que se integra armoniosamente en el paisaje.

Nel 1989 il commerciante di vini Agustin Huneeus e sua moglie Valeria scoprirono uno degli ultimi terreni della Napa Valley che ancora non fosse sfruttato per la viticoltu-ra. Riusciti ad acquistare la proprietà, dall'estensione di circa 113 ettari, vi fondarono una nuova tenuta vitivinicola: Quintessa. Il nome fa riferimento a cinque inconfondibili colline comprese nel territorio della tenuta, ma anche all'ambizioso obiettivo di produrre vini "quintessenziali". La cantina di vinificazione sotterranea, completata nel 2002, è delimitata da un caratteristico muro in pietra naturale dalla forma a falce, grazie al quale il complesso s'inserisce armonicamente nel paesaggio circostante.

Agustin & Valeria Huneeus,
proprietors of Quintessa

Agustin & Valeria Huneeus,
Eigentümer von Quintessa

Agustin & Valeria Huneeus,
propriétaires de Quintessa

Agustin & Valeria Huneeus,
propietarios de Quintessa

Agustin & Valeria Huneeus,
proprietari di Quintessa

20 Quintessa *California, USA*

With their use of high-quality materials and *careful detail planning, Walker Warner Architects have carried on the quality philosophy of Quintessa in the architecture of the winery estate.*

Durch die Verwendung hochwertiger Materialien *und eine sensible Detailplanung setzten Walker Warner Architects die Qualitätsphilosophie von Quintessa in der Architektur des Weingutes fort.*

L'utilisation de matériaux de haute qualité *et la conception des détails toute en finesse, voulues par Walker Warner Architects, traduisent la philosophie de la qualité de Quintessa dans l'architecture du domaine.*

Con el empleo de materiales costosos *y una sensible planificación de los detalles, Walker Warner Architects han seguido la filosofía de calidad de Quintessa también en la arquitectura de sus bodegas.*

Utilizzando materiali di gran pregio *e un'attenta pianificazione dei dettagli, gli architetti della Walker Warner Architects hanno trasformato in architettura la filosofia della qualità che ispira Quintessa.*

Rubicon Estate
California, USA

Finnish sailor Gustave Niebaum founded this winery in 1880 under the name "Inglenook". It only took him ten years to produce wines that can hold their own among any of the top European products. Niebaum's great nephew John Daniels, Jr. then continued this tradition. However, a lack of financial success forced him to sell off large parts of the winery estate. In 1975, film director Francis Ford Coppola committed himself to reuniting the original property. Since 2006, the winery has been operating as Rubicon Estate—named after its best wine.

Das Weingut wurde 1880 durch den finnischen Seemann Gustave Niebaum unter dem Namen „Inglenook" gegründet. Es gelang ihm, innerhalb von nur 10 Jahren Weine zu erzeugen, die keinen Vergleich mit europäischen Spitzenprodukten zu scheuen brauchten. Später setzte Niebaums Großneffe John Daniels jr. diese Tradition fort. Mangelnder finanzieller Erfolg zwang ihn jedoch zum Verkauf großer Teile des Weingutes. 1975 machte es sich Filmregisseur Francis Ford Coppola zur Aufgabe, den ursprünglichen Besitz wieder zu vereinen. Seit 2006 firmiert das Weingut – benannt nach seinem Spitzenwein – als Rubicon Estate.

Le domaine fut créé en 1880 par le marin finlandais Gustave Niebaum sous le nom d'« Inglenook ». En l'espace de seulement 10 ans, il réussit à produire des vins qui rivalisaient aisément avec les produits européens de qualité supérieure. Ultérieurement, le petit-neveu de Niebaum, John Daniels Jr., perpétua cette tradition. Cependant, des déboires financiers le contraignirent à vendre de grandes parties du domaine. En 1975, le metteur en scène Francis Ford Coppola se chargea de réunir la propriété d'origine. Depuis 2006, le domaine opère sous le nom de son meilleur vin, Rubicon Estate.

La bodega fue fundada en 1880 por el marinero finlandés Gustave Niebaum con el nombre "Inglenook". En el breve plazo de 10 años éste fue capaz de concebir vinos muy a la altura de los grandes caldos europeos. Posteriormente sería John Daniels jr., sobrino nieto de Niebaum, quien continuara tal tradición. En 1975 el director de cine Francis Ford Coppola se hizo con la misión de reunir la propiedad original. Desde 2006 la bodega lleva el nombre de su gran vino: Rubicon Estate.

La tenuta fu fondata nel 1880 dal marinaio finlandese Gustave Niebaum, che le diede il nome di "Inglenook" e nell'arco di soli dieci anni riuscì a produrre vini che non temevano il confronto con i migliori prodotti europei. Successivamente, a mantenere viva questa tradizione fu il pronipote di Niebaum, John Daniels jr., che però a causa dello scarso successo economico si vide costretto a vendere gran parte della tenuta. Nel 1975 il regista cinematografico Francis Ford Coppola decise di tentare di riunificare la proprietà originaria: dal 2006 la tenuta è stata ribattezzata Rubicon Estate dal nome del suo vino più prestigioso.

Francis Ford Coppola,
proprietor of Rubicon Estate

Francis Ford Coppola,
Eigentümer von Rubicon Estate

Francis Ford Coppola,
propriétaire de Rubicon Estate

Francis Ford Coppola,
propietario de Rubicon Estate

Francis Ford Coppola,
proprietario di Rubicon Estate

Château Beychevelle

Saint-Julien, Bordeaux, France

This majestic castle was erected in the 17th Century and received its current shape in 1757. Its name is derived from the French expression "baisse voile": One of its earlier owners was Jean-Louis Nogaret de la Valette, Great Admiral and Governor of the Guyenne, who was so powerful that passing ships had to haul down their sails as a sign of respect. The winery estate produces the Grand Cru Classé Château Beychevelle as well as its "little brothers" Amiral de Beychevelle and Les Brulières de Beychevelle.

Das herrschaftliche Schloss wurde im 17. Jahrhundert errichtet und erhielt 1757 seine heutige Gestalt. Sein Name geht auf den französischen Ausdruck „baisse voile" zurück: Einer der früheren Besitzer war Jean-Louis Nogaret de la Valette, Großadmiral und Gouverneur der Guyenne, dessen Machtfülle so gewaltig war, dass vorbeifahrende Schiffe als Zeichen der Gefolgschaft die Segel streichen mussten. Das Weingut produziert den Grand Cru Classé Château Beychevelle sowie dessen „kleine Brüder" Amiral de Beychevelle und Les Brulières de Beychevelle.

Le château seigneurial fut construit au 17ème siècle et la modification de 1757 lui donna son apparence actuelle. Son nom vient de l'expression française « baisse voile » : l'un de ses anciens propriétaires était Jean-Louis Nogaret de la Valette, grand amiral et gouverneur de Guyenne et sa puissance était telle que les navires passant au large du domaine devaient baisser les voiles en signe d'allégeance. Le domaine produit le Grand Cru Classé Château Beychevelle ainsi que ses « petits frères », Amiral de Beychevelle et Les Brulières de Beychevelle.

El castillo señorial fue construido en el siglo XVII y en 1757 adoptó su forma actual. Su nombre proviene de la expresión francesa "baisse voile": Uno de sus primeros propietarios fue Jean-Louis Nogaret de la Valette, gran almirante y gobernador de la Aquitania, y con tal poder que aquellos barcos que cruzaran aguas de su territorio debían plegar las velas en señal de sumisión. Las bodegas producen el Grand Cru Classé Château Beychevelle y sus "hermanos menores" Amiral de Beychevelle y Les Brulières de Beychevelle.

Il signorile castello, edificato nel XVII secolo, si è conservato nella sua forma attuale sin dal 1757. Il suo nome deriva dall'espressione francese "baisse voile": uno dei suoi proprietari del passato fu infatti Jean-Louis Nogaret de la Valette, grande ammiraglio e governatore dell'Aquitania, il cui potere era tale che le navi di passaggio in segno di devozione erano tenute ad abbassare le vele. La tenuta vinicola produce il Grand Cru Classé Château Beychevelle, ma anche i suoi "fratelli minori" Amiral de Beychevelle e Les Brulières de Beychevelle.

Philippe Blanc, *General Manager of Château Beychevelle*

Philippe Blanc, *Geschäftsführer von Château Beychevelle*

Philippe Blanc, *Directeur Général du Château Beychevelle*

Philippe Blanc, *director gerente de Château Beychevelle*

Philippe Blanc, *amministratore delegato di Château Beychevelle*

CHÂTEAU BEYCHEVELLE

GRAND VIN 2003

— SAINT-JULIEN —

During recent decades, *Château Beychevelle has relied on longer mashing times and on the increased use of new Barriques, which are stored in long rows in the maturity cellars of the winery.*

In den letzten Jahrzehnten *setzte Château Beychevelle auf längere Maischezeiten und den verstärkten Einsatz von neuen Barriques, die in langen Reihen in den Reifekellern des Weinguts lagern.*

Ces dernières décennies, *le Château Beychevelle a misé sur un temps de cuvage plus long et mis l'accent sur l'emploi de nouvelles barriques, entreposées en longues rangées dans les caves de maturation du domaine.*

En las últimas décadas *el Château Beychevelle se ha centrado en periodos más prolongados de fermentación del mosto y en la introducción de nuevas barricas, que se almacenan en largas hileras dentro de las bodegas de crianza.*

Negli ultimi decenni *Château Beychevelle ha puntato su prolungati tempi di macerazione del mosto e su un più ampio impiego di nuove barrique, conservate in lunghe file nelle cantine di maturazione della tenuta.*

The lavish and luxurious atmosphere of the Château bears powerful testimony to the century-old affluence of the winery estate. It is not considered one of the most beautiful estates of the Médoc for nothing.

Das großzügige und luxuriöse Ambiente des Châteaus legt ein eindrucksvolles Zeugnis vom jahrhundertealten Wohlstand des Weingutes ab. Nicht umsonst gilt es als eines der schönsten Güter des Médoc.

L'atmosphère opulente et luxueuse du château livre un témoignage impressionnant de plusieurs siècles de prospérité du domaine. C'est une des raisons pour lesquelles il passe pour l'un des plus beaux domaines du Médoc.

El generoso y lujoso ambiente del Château da testimonio de los siglos de bienestar que vivió la bodega. De ahí que se considere una de las propiedades más bellas de Médoc.

Gli ambienti riccamente decorati e lussuosi del Castello sono la prova evidente della secolare ricchezza dell'azienda vinicola, che non a caso è considerata una delle più belle in tutto il Médoc.

Château Talbot

Saint-Julien, Bordeaux, France

Its name is probably derived from John Talbot, the last British commander of Aquitaine and whose connection to the estate has yet to be established. Since 1917, the winery has been in the estate of the Cordier family. It includes more than 247 acres of excellent acreage stretching from the Gironde inland all the way behind Saint-Julien-Beychevelle, to the north of Gruaud Larose. Inside the Château, historic furniture and wall panels blend with subtle modern additions into an original and harmonïous unit.

Der Name geht wahrscheinlich zurück auf den letzten englischen Befehlshaber von Aquitanien, John Talbot, dessen genaue Verbindung mit dem Gut jedoch nicht geklärt ist. Seit 1917 ist das Weingut im Besitz der Familie Cordier. Zum ihm gehören über 100 ha exzellente Anbauflächen, die sich von der Gironde aus landeinwärts bis hinter Saint-Julien-Beychevelle, nördlich von Gruaud Larose erstrecken. In den Innenräumen des Châteaus verbinden sich historische Möbel und Wandverkleidungen mit subtilen modernen Einbauten zu einer originellen und harmonische Einheit.

Le nom vient probablement du dernier connétable anglais d'Aquitaine, John Talbot, dont le lien exact avec le domaine n'est cependant pas clair. Depuis 1917, la famille Cordier est propriétaire du domaine. Il compte plus d'une centaine d'hectares de sols excellents, qui s'étendent de la Gironde vers l'intérieur des terres jusqu'à Saint-Julien-Beychevelle, au nord de Gruaud Larose. Dans les intérieurs du château, les meubles et les lambris historiques côtoient de subtiles menuiseries modernes et forment un ensemble original et harmonieux.

Probablemente el nombre se remonte al último comandante de Aquitania, John Talbot, si bien no se sabe con certeza cuál fue su relación con la propiedad. Desde 1917 la bodega pertenece a la familia Cordier. El dominio está formado por 100 excelentes hectáreas de cultivo que se extienden por el Gironda hacia el interior hasta Saint-Julien-Beychevelle, al norte de Gruaud Larose. En el interior del Château la decoración vincula muebles históricos y revestimientos murales con sutiles modernas construcciones creando una unidad armoniosa y original.

Il nome Château Talbot risale probabilmente all'ultimo comandante inglese in Aquitania, John Talbot, anche se non è chiaro quale fosse il suo effettivo legame con la tenuta. La famiglia Cordier è proprietaria dal 1917 dell'azienda vinicola, di cui fan parte più di 100 ettari di eccellenti vigneti che si estendono dalla Gironda verso l'entroterra fino a dietro Saint-Julien-Beychevelle, a nord di Gruaud Larose. Negli interni del castello, mobili antichi e rivestimenti parietali si alternano a sottili inserti moderni creando un'unità originale ed armoniosa.

Nancy Bignon, co-owner of Château Talbot with her sister Lorraine Rustmann

Nancy Bignon, gemeinsam mit ihrer Schwester Lorraine Rustmann Besitzerin von Château Talbot

Nancy Bignon, copropriétaire avec sa sœur Lorraine Rustmann du Château Talbot

Nancy Bignon, copropietaria de Château Talbot junto con su hermana Lorraine Rustmann

Nancy Bignon, comproprietaria di Château Talbot insieme alla sorella Lorraine Rustmann

This winery estate applies the latest research of the Ecole Bordelaise d'Œnologie. As a result, the wines are always produced and matured in new barrels.

Das Weingut arbeitet nach den neuesten Erkenntnissen der Ecole Bordelaise d'Œnologie. Entsprechend finden Herstellung und Reife der Weine grundsätzlich in neuen Fässern statt.

Le domaine met en œuvre les connaissances les plus récentes de l'Ecole Bordelaise d'Œnologie. En conséquence, la fabrication et la maturation des vins s'effectuent fondamentalement dans des fûts neufs.

La bodega trabaja según las últimas teorías de la Ecole Bordelaise d'Œnologie; por ello, la elaboración y crianza de los vinos tiene lugar fundamentalmente en barricas nuevas.

L'azienda vinicola lavora seguendo i più moderni dettami della ricerca enologica dell'Ecole Bordelaise d'Œnologie: per questo motivo, la produzione e la maturazione dei vini hanno luogo per una scelta di principio in botti nuove.

Everything must change in order for nothing to change. In line with this expression, the historic rooms reveal discretely added renovations—if you look closely.

Alles muss sich wandeln, damit es bleiben kann, wie es ist. Getreu diesem Motto finden sich in den historischen Räumen — bei genauem Hinsehen — behutsam eingefügte Neuerungen.

Il faut que tout change afin que rien ne change. Pour illustrer cette devise, on trouve dans les pièces historiques du château — en y regardant de plus près — des innovations savamment intégrées.

Todo debe transformarse para que continúe siendo como es. Un lema que mantienen fielmente los salones históricos, en los que si se mira detenidamente, sí se encuentran elementos nuevos insertados cuidadosamente.

Parafrasando il Gattopardo, tutto deve cambiare, perchè nulla cambi: questo il motto messo in pratica nelle sale storiche, in cui uno sguardo attento scoprirà innovazioni inserite con cautela.

Château du Tertre

Margaux, Bordeaux, France

Surrounded by a sea of grapevine, the Château du Tertre lies between the villages of Arsac and Ligondras on one of the highest elevations of the Appellation Margaux. During the course of the centuries, it changed owners multiple times. One of these was Pierre Mitchell, the first bottle producer in Bordeaux, in the 18th Century. Laid out in strictly symmetrical fashion, this elegant estate presents itself perfectly renovated today. The winery too has been undergoing modernization since 1995 under the new owner, Eric Albada Jelgersma.

Umgeben von einem Meer aus Weinreben liegt das Château du Tertre zwischen den Orten Arsac und Ligondras auf einer der höchsten Erhebungen der Appellation Margaux. Im Laufe der Jahrhunderte wechselten mehrfach die Besitzer; unter ihnen war im 18. Jahrhundert auch Pierre Mitchell, der erste Flaschenproduzent im Bordeaux. Das streng symmetrisch angelegte, elegante Gutshaus präsentiert sich heute perfekt renoviert, und auch das Weingut erlebte seit 1995 unter dem neuen Besitzer Eric Albada Jelgersma einen Modernisierungsschub.

Entouré d'un océan de vignes, le Château du Tertre trône entre les villages d'Arsac et de Ligondras, sur l'un des plus hauts coteaux de l'appellation Margaux. Les propriétaires se sont succédé au fil des siècles ; il se trouva aussi parmi eux, au 18ème siècle, Pierre Mitchell, le premier producteur de bouteilles à Bordeaux. L'élégant manoir, construit dans une stricte symétrie, a fait peau neuve et tout le domaine a d'ailleurs fait l'objet, depuis 1995, d'une importante modernisation à l'initiative du nouveau propriétaire, Eric Albada Jelgersma.

Entre Arsac y Ligondras, en una de las mayores elevaciones de la zona de apelación Margaux se levanta Château du Tertre, circundado por un mar de viñedos. A lo largo de los siglos sus propietarios cambiaron en diversas ocasiones; uno de ellos fue en el siglo XVIII Pierre Mitchell, el primer productor de botellas de Burdeos. La elegante casa señorial emplazada con una estricta simetría ha sido en la actualidad completamente renovada, así como toda la propiedad, que desde 1995 viene siendo modernizada por su nuevo propietario, Eric Albada Jelgersma.

Immerso in un mare di vigneti, Château du Tertre si erge tra le località di Arsac e Ligondras su una delle alture più elevate dell'Appellation Margaux. Nel corso dei secoli vi si sono avvicendati numerosi proprietari, tra cui, nel XVIII secolo, anche Pierre Mitchell, il primo produttore di vini in bottiglia del Bordeaux. L'elegante castello, dalla severa disposizione simmetrica, è stato recentemente restaurato, e a partire dal 1995 anche la tenuta vinicola, grazie all'impegno del nuovo proprietario, Eric Albada Jelgersma, ha vissuto una nuova fase di modernizzazione.

Eric Albada Jelgersma, president of the SE Château Giscours and owner of Château du Tertre

Eric Albada Jelgersma, Präsident der SE Château Giscours und Eigentümer von Château du Tertre

Eric Albada Jelgersma, Président de la SE du Château Giscours et propriétaire du Château du Tertre

Eric Albada Jelgersma, presidente de SE Château Giscours y propietario de Château du Tertre

Eric Albada Jelgersma, presidente della SE Château Giscours e proprietario di Château du Tertre

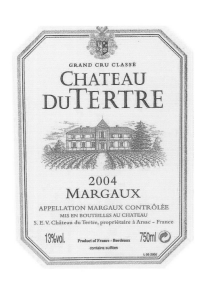

The tastefully furnished degustation rooms distinguish themselves with soft, harmoniously balanced colors.

Die geschmackvoll eingerichteten Degustationsräume werden von sanften, harmonisch abgestimmten Farben geprägt.

Les salles de dégustation aménagées avec goût sont marquées par des couleurs douces parfaitement harmonisées.

Las exquisitas salas de catas están envueltas en tonos suaves y armónicos.

I locali destinati alla degustazione dei vini, arredati con gusto, si distinguono per il cromatismo dolce e armonioso della decorazione.

Whereas the living quarters of the Château emanate dignified upper-class sophistication, the degustation rooms are characterized by their timeless, simple elegance.

Während die Wohnräume des Châteaus großbürgerliche Gediegenheit ausstrahlen, zeichnen sich die Degustationsräume durch zeitlose, schlichte Eleganz aus.

Tandis que les pièces d'habitation du château respirent l'aisance de la grande bourgeoisie, les salles de dégustation se distinguent par une élégance intemporelle et sobre.

Mientras que los espacios de vivienda del Château irradian la pureza de la alta burguesía, las salas de catas se caracterizan por una elegancia austera y atemporal.

Mentre negli interni del castello si respira la solida atmosfera altoborghese, i locali destinati alla degustazione si distinguono per la loro eleganza classica e sobria.

Château Giscour

Margaux, Bordeaux, France

Due in no small part to its relatively large acreage of 198 acres, the Château is among the best known wineries of the Appellation Margaux. Listed for the first time as a winery in 1552, the Château was categorized as a 3e Cru classé in an 1855 classification. Several changes in ownership then led to a decline of the Château. It wasn't until it was purchased by Nicolas Tari that the winery regained its old splendor after World War II. Today, it's owned by Dutchman Eric Albada Jelgersma—just like the Château du Tertre.

Das Château zählt – nicht zuletzt aufgrund seiner relativ großen Anbauflächen von 80 ha – zu den bekanntesten Gütern der Appellation Margaux. 1552 wurde das Château erstmals als Weingut erwähnt, die Klassifikation von 1855 stufte es als 3e Cru classé ein. Mehrere Besitzerwechsel führten danach zu einem Niedergang des Châteaus. Erst nach dem Kauf durch Nicolas Tari stieg das Gut nach dem 2. Weltkrieg wieder zu alter Größe auf. Heute befindet es sich – wie auch das Château du Tertre – im Besitz des Holländers Eric Albada Jelgersma.

Le Château Giscours compte parmi les domaines les plus renommés de l'appellation Margaux, en raison, entre autres, d'un vignoble relativement étendu de 80 hectares. Le Château est cité comme domaine viticole pour la première fois en 1552, et la classification de 1855 le classa 3ème Cru Classé. Plusieurs changements de propriétaires causèrent son déclin. Ce n'est qu'après son rachat par Nicolas Tari que le domaine retrouva, après la 2ème guerre mondiale, son ancienne gloire. Il est aujourd'hui – tout comme le Château du Tertre – aux mains du Néerlandais Eric Albada Jelgersma.

El Château está considerado uno de los dominios más conocidos de la apelación de Margaux, en parte también por su relativamente gran superficie de cultivo de 80 hectáreas. Como bodega se le mencionaba por primera vez en 1552, y más tarde, la clasificación de 1855 lo situaría en la posición de tercer Cru classé. Los diversos cambios de propietario lo llevaron al ocaso, y hubo que esperar hasta que lo adquiriera Nicolas Tari, tras la Segunda Guerra Mundial, para que la propiedad viviera una recuperación y alcanzara de nuevo su tamaño original. Hoy, al igual que el Château du Tertre, pertenece al holandés Eric Albada Jelgersma.

Anche per i suoi ottanta ettari di vigneti, un'estensione piuttosto considerevole, Château Giscours è una delle aziende vinicole più rinomate dell'Appellation Margaux. Citato per la prima volta come tenuta vinicola nel 1552, in occasione della Classificazione del 1855 ottenne il titolo ufficiale di 3e Cru classé. In seguito a numerosi cambi di proprietà la tenuta subì poi un periodo di decadenza, da cui si riprese solo dopo la Seconda Guerra Mondiale, quando Nicolas Tari la acquistò riportandola agli antichi splendori. Oggi il castello, come del resto anche Château du Tertre, è proprietà dell'olandese Eric Albada Jelgersma.

A view into the cellars at Château Giscours.

Ein Blick in den Fasskeller von *Château Giscours.*

Vue sur le chai du *Château Giscours.*

Un vistazo en la sala de barricas de *Château Giscours.*

Un'occhiata alla cantina d'invecchiamento di *Château Giscours.*

Château Palmer

Margaux, Bordeaux, France

In the early 19th Century, Englishman Charles Palmer purchased an already existing winery and expanded it with a lot of time, energy and money. Regrettably, his passion outgrew his financial means—Palmer had to sell the winery estate in 1843. In 1856, the Château with its representative façades and elegant salons was built by the Péreire, its new owners, as a combination of classicism, baroque and renaissance. In 1938, they sold the winery to several French, English and Dutch wine merchant families, whose heirs operate it today.

Der Engländer Charles Palmer erwarb im frühen 19. Jahrhundert ein bereits bestehendes Weingut und erweiterte es unter hohem Einsatz an Zeit, Energie und Geld. Seine Leidenschaft überstieg allerdings die finanziellen Mittel – 1843 musste Palmer das Weingut verkaufen. Das Château mit seinen repräsentativen Fassaden und stilvollen Salons wurde 1856 von den neuen Besitzern Péreire in einer Mischung aus Klassizismus, Barock- und Renaissanceelementen errichtet. Sie verkauften das Gut 1938 an mehrere französische, englische und holländische Weinhändlerfamilien, deren Erben es heute weiterführen.

L'Anglais Charles Palmer fit l'acquisition, au début du 19ème siècle, du domaine existant et l'étendit en déployant beaucoup de temps, d'énergie et d'argent. Malheureusement, sa passion dépassait ses moyens financiers et Palmer dut céder le domaine en 1843. Le château, avec ses façades représentatives et ses salons élégants, fut construit en 1856 par les nouveaux propriétaires, les Péreire, et mêle des éléments du Classicisme, du Baroque et de la Renaissance. Ceux-ci revendirent le domaine en 1938 à plusieurs familles de négociants en vins françaises, anglaises et hollandaises, dont les héritiers en assurent aujourd'hui la gestion.

A principios del siglo XIX el inglés Charles Palmer adquirió las bodegas ya existentes y las amplió realizando una enorme inversión de trabajo, energía y dinero. Sin embargo, su pasión estaba muy por encima de sus medios financieros, y en 1843 Palmer tuvo que vender la propiedad. En 1856 sus nuevos propietarios, Péreire, construyeron el Château con su representativa fachada y sus refinados salones, como fusión de elementos clasicistas, barrocos y renacentistas. En 1938 vendieron la propiedad a diversas familias de bodegueros francesas, inglesas y holandesas, cuyos herederos continúan hoy dirigiéndola.

Agli inizi del XIX secolo l'inglese Charles Palmer acquistò la tenuta vinicola preesistente e l'ampliò con grande dispendio di tempo, energia e denaro. Purtroppo però la sua passione superò i limiti delle risorse finanziarie disponibili, tanto che nel 1843 Palmer dovette vendere. Nel 1856 i nuovi proprietari, di nome Péreire, fecero costruire Il castello dalle prestigiose facciate e dagli eleganti saloni, in uno stile che mescola elementi neoclassici, barocchi e rinascimentali; nel 1938 la tenuta fu rivenduta a diverse famiglie di commercianti vinicoli francesi, inglesi e olandesi, i cui eredi sono ancora oggi alla guida dell'azienda.

Thomas Duroux,
Director of Château Palmer

Thomas Duroux,
Geschäftsführer des Château Palmer

Thomas Duroux,
Directeur Général du Château Palmer

Thomas Duroux,
director gerente de Château Palmer

Thomas Duroux,
direttore di Château Palmer

Château Palmer *Margaux, Bordeaux, France*

While the interior of the castle still radiates the charm of the time of its construction, its garden has only been established in recent times as a topiary garden with delicately groomed ornamental bushes.

Während die Innenräume des Schlosses noch den Charme der Erbauungszeit versprühen, wurde der Garten erst in jüngster Zeit als Topiari-Garten mit kunstvoll beschnittenen Ziergehölzen angelegt.

Tandis que les intérieurs du château sont encore embués du charme des débuts, le parc a été aménagé il y a peu en jardin topiaire avec des bosquets décoratifs artistiquement taillés.

Mientras que los interiores del castillo aún emanan el encanto de los tiempos de su fundación, el jardín ha sido concebido recientemente como un jardín topiario con arbustos ornamentales podados artísticamente.

Mentre negli interni del castello si respira ancora il fascino della sua epoca d'origine, il giardino è stato allestito solo di recente seguendo i dettami dell'arte topiaria, con arbusti ornamentali ad arte.

Château Latour

Pauillac, Bordeaux, France

The name of this winery refers to a 14th Century observation tower that once overlooked the mouth of the Gironde. That tower, however, has vanished completely and has nothing to do with the prominent round tower standing amidst the vineyards today. Since the 17th Century, the winery had belonged to the estate of the Ségur family that gave it its great reputation. In 1993, François Pinault, entrepreneur and billionaire, purchased Château Latour. The "Grand Vin" of the winery is exclusively derived from vines, which are up to 100 years old and which grow in the "Enclos" around the Château.

Der Name des Weingutes bezieht sich auf einen Beobachtungsturm aus dem 14. Jahrhundert, der einst die Mündung der Gironde überblickte. Dieser Turm ist jedoch spurlos verschwunden und hat nichts mit dem markanten Rundturm zu tun, der heute inmitten der Weinberge steht. Seit dem 17. Jahrhundert war das Weingut im Besitz der Familie Ségur, unter der es seinen großen Ruf erlangte. 1993 erwarb schließlich der Unternehmer und Milliardär François Pinault Château Latour. Der „Grand Vin" des Weinguts wird ausschließlich aus den zum Teil 100-jährigen Reben gewonnen, die im „Enclos" rund um das Château wachsen.

Le nom du domaine fait référence à une tour d'observation du 14ème siècle, dominant jadis l'estuaire de la Gironde. Cette tour a disparu sans laisser de trace et n'a rien à voir avec l'imposante tour circulaire qui se dresse aujourd'hui au cœur des vignes. Depuis le 17ème siècle, le domaine était la propriété de la famille Ségur, qui l'amena à sa grande notoriété. En 1993, l'homme d'affaires et milliardaire François Pinault acquit le Château Latour. Le « Grand Vin » du domaine est produit exclusivement à partir des ceps, centenaires pour certains, qui poussent dans l'« Enclos » autour du château.

Las bodegas deben su nombre a una torre de observación del siglo XIV, que en su día divisaba el estuario de Gironda. La torre real, sin embargo, desapareció sin dejar rastro y no tiene nada que ver con la imponente torre que hoy se levanta en el centro de los viñedos. Desde el siglo XVII las bodegas fueron propiedad de la familia Ségur, bajo la que adquirieron su gran fama. En 1993 el empresario y millonario François Pinault adquirió Château Latour. El "Grand Vin" de estas bodegas se obtiene exclusivamente de las cepas que crecen en el "enclos" en torno al Château, algunas de ellas con más de 100 años.

Il nome della tenuta si rifà a una torre di guardia, costruita nel XIV secolo per sorvegliare l'estuario della Gironda, la quale però è scomparsa senza lasciare tracce e non ha nulla a che fare con il caratteristico torrione rotondo che ora campeggia in mezzo ai vigneti. Giunto a grande celebrità sotto la guida della famiglia Ségur, cui appartenne fin dal XVII secolo, nel 1993 Château Latour è stato acquistato dall'imprenditore e miliardario François Pinault. Il "Grand Vin" della tenuta si ricava esclusivamente dai vitigni in parte centenari che crescono nell'"Enclos" intorno al castello.

François Pinault, proprietor of *Château Latour*

François Pinault, der Eigentümer von *Château Latour*

François Pinault, propriétaire du *Château Latour*

François Pinault, propietario de *Château Latour*

François Pinault, proprietario di *Château Latour*

Château Latour   *Pauillac, Bordeaux, France*

This traditional winery surprises its visitors with a stylish, almost minimalist degustation room. Ultra-modern stainless steel tanks were applied in its fermentation cellar as early as the mid-1960s.

Das Traditionsweingut überrascht seine Besucher mit einem schicken, beinahe minimalistisch gestalteten Degustationsraum. Schon seit Mitte der 60er-Jahre wird im Gärkeller mit hochmodernen Edelstahltanks gearbeitet.

Ce domaine viticole de tradition surprend ses visiteurs avec une salle de dégustation chic, à l'aménagement quasi minimaliste. Dès le milieu des années 60, on a commencé à travailler avec des cuves en inox ultramodernes dans la cave de fermentation.

Estas bodegas de tradición sorprenden a sus visitantes con una sala de catas refinada y casi minimalista. En la sala de elaboración se trabaja con modernos depósitos de acero inoxidable desde mediados de los años 60.

L'azienda vinicola di lunga tradizione sorprende i suoi visitatori con una sala di degustazione chic, dall'arredamento quasi minimalista. Già dalla metà degli anni Sessanta nella cantina di fermentazione si lavora con modernissimi serbatoi in acciaio inox.

Château Latour   Pauillac, Bordeaux, France   51

Château Pichon-Longueville

Pauillac, Bordeaux, France

Jacques de Pichon, Baron de Longueville, established the tradition of the Pichon-Longueville winery in the 17th Century, which also included the estate of the present neighboring winery Pichon-Lalande until the mid-19th Century. Following the distribution of the estate, his descendent Raoul de Pichon used his portion of the inheritance to establish the Château in its present form in 1851. Since 1987, the castle and winery have been part of the estate of the insurance group AXA Millésimes. The latter has meticulously restored the castle and erected a new production facility, whose architecture harmoniously blends in with the historic ensemble.

Jacques de Pichon, Baron de Longueville, begründete im 17. Jahrhundert die Tradition des Weingutes Pichon-Longueville, zudem bis zur Mitte des 19. Jahrhunderts auch der Besitz des jetzigen Nachbargutes Pichon-Lalande gehörte. Nach Erbteilung errichtete sein Nachkomme Raoul de Pichon auf dem ihm zugefallenen Teil 1851 das Château in seiner heutigen Form. Seit 1987 sind Schloss und Weingut im Besitz des Versicherungskonzerns AXA Millésimes. Diese hat das Schloss aufwendig saniert sowie ein neues Produktionsgebäude errichtet, dessen Architektur sich harmonisch in das historische Ensemble einfügt.

Jacques de Pichon, baron de Longueville, fonda au 17ème siècle la tradition du domaine Pichon-Longueville auquel appartenait aussi, jusqu'au milieu du 19ème siècle, l'actuel domaine voisin de Pichon-Lalande. A la suite de la scission par héritage, son descendant Raoul de Pichon fit construire, en 1851, le château tel qu'il existe aujourd'hui sur la parcelle qui lui revint. Depuis 1987, le château et le domaine sont aux mains de la compagnie d'assurances AXA Millésimes. Celle-ci a fait rénover le château à grands frais et construire un nouveau bâtiment de production dont l'architecture se fond harmonieusement dans l'ensemble historique.

En el siglo XVII Jacques de Pichon, barón de Longueville, fundó las bodegas Pichon-Longueville, a las que hasta mediados del siglo XIX también pertenecieron los viñedos vecinos Pichon-Lalande. Tras la repartición de la herencia en 1851, su sucesor, Raoul de Pichon, construyó el castillo en su forma actual. Desde 1987 el castillo y las bodegas son propiedad del grupo AXA Millésimes de seguros. La empresa se ha encargado de sanearlas a fondo y de construir un nuevo edificio de producción dotado de una arquitectura que se funde armoniosamente en el conjunto histórico.

Nel XVII secolo Jacques de Pichon, Barone de Longueville, diede inizio alla grande tradizione della tenuta di Pichon-Longueville, cui fino alla metà del XIX secolo apparteneva anche la proprietà dell'attuale vicina Pichon-Lalande. Una volta spartita l'eredità, nel 1851 il suo discendente Raoul de Pichon fece costruire sulla parte a lui spettante il castello nella sua forma attuale. Dal 1987 sia il castello che l'azienda vinicola appartengono al Gruppo Assicurativo AXA Millésimes, il quale ha proceduto ad un completo restauro del castello e a far costruire una nuova cantina di vinificazione, la cui architettura viene a integrarsi con armonia nell'insieme storico della tenuta.

Christian Seely, *Managing director of AXA Millésimes*

Christian Seely, *Geschäftsführer von AXA Millésimes*

Christian Seely, *Directeur Général d'AXA Millésimes*

Christian Seely, *director gerente de AXA Millésimes*

Christian Seely, *direttore generale di AXA Millésimes*

54   Château Pichon-Longueville   *Pauillac, France*

Château Haut-Bailly

Pessac-Léognan, Bordeaux, France

A banker named Le Bailly founded this winery in 1630. However, it wasn't until Alcide Bellot de Minières purchased the estate in 1872 that Haut-Bailly acquired the size and significance it enjoys today. De Minières was both a clever businessman and a highly talented winegrower—his knowledge and success even earned him the praise "King of Wines" among his contemporaries. In 1955, the estate went to Daniel Sanders. Today, his granddaughter manages the Château, which has been owned by American banker Robert G. Wilmers since 1998.

Gegründet wurde das Weingut im Jahre 1630 von einem Bankier namens Le Bailly. Erst mit dem Kauf des Besitzes durch Alcide Bellot de Minières im Jahre 1872 erlangte Haut-Bailly jedoch seine heutige Größe und Bedeutung. De Minières war sowohl ein geschickter Kaufmann, als auch ein hochtalentierter Winzer – seine Zeitgenossen nannten ihn aufgrund seiner Kenntnisse und Erfolge gar „König des Weines". 1955 gelangte das Gut an Daniel Sanders. Seine Enkelin ist heute die Verwalterin des Châteaus, das sich seit 1998 im Besitz des amerikanischen Bankiers Robert G. Wilmers befindet.

Le domaine fut fondé en 1630 par un banquier nommé Le Bailly. Mais c'est seulement quand il fut racheté par Alcide Bellot de Minières en 1872 que le Haut-Bailly acquit sa taille et son importance actuelle. De Minières était non seulement un habile marchand mais aussi un talentueux vigneron – ses contemporains l'appelaient même le « roi du vin » en raison de ses connaissances et de ses succès. En 1955, Daniel Sanders entra en possession du domaine. Sa petite-fille est aujourd'hui l'administratrice du château dont le banquier américain Robert G. Wilmers est propriétaire depuis 1998.

En 1630 un banquero llamado Le Bailly fundó los viñedos. Pero Haut-Bailly tuvo que esperar hasta 1872, al ser comprado por Alcide Bellot de Minières, para alcanzar el tamaño e importancia que comporta hoy. De Minières no sólo era un audaz comerciante sino también un viticultor con talento, de ahí que en su época fuera conocido como el "rey del vino" por sus conocimientos y éxito en este campo. En 1955 la propiedad pasó a manos de Daniel Sanders. Su nieta es hoy la administradora del Château, que desde 1998 pertenece al banquero americano Robert G. Wilmers.

L'azienda vinicola fu fondata nel 1630 da un banchiere, un certo Le Bailly, ma solo nel 1872, quando ne divenne proprietario Alcide Bellot de Minières, Haut-Bailly raggiunse la sua attuale grandezza e importanza. De Minières infatti non era solo un abile uomo d'affari, ma anche un viticoltore di grande talento: a causa delle sue conoscenze e dei successi da lui raccolti i contemporanei lo chiamavano "il re del vino". Nel 1955 la tenuta passò a Daniel Sanders, la cui nipote oggi amministra il castello, divenuto dal 1998 proprietà del banchiere americano Robert G. Wilmers.

Robert G. Wilmers, *proprietor of Château Haut-Bailly*

Robert G. Wilmers, *Eigentümer von Château Haut-Bailly*

Robert G. Wilmers, *propriétaire du Château Haut-Bailly*

Robert G. Wilmers, *propietario de Château Haut-Bailly*

Robert G. Wilmers, *proprietario di Château Haut-Bailly*

GRAND VIN DE BORDEAUX

CHATEAU HAUT-BAILLY

GRAND CRU CLASSÉ

PESSAC-LÉOGNAN

2003

MIS EN BOUTEILLE AU CHATEAU

The castle, whose structure had deteriorated during time, today stands fully renovated. The production sites of the winery have undergone meticulous modernization as well.

Das Schloss, das zwischenzeitlich in baulich schlechtem Zustand war, präsentiert sich heute umfassend saniert. Auch die Produktionsanlagen des Weingutes wurden aufwendig modernisiert.

Le Château, qui fut pendant un certain temps en piteux état, a entièrement fait peau neuve. Les installations de production du domaine ont également bénéficié d'une modernisation de grande envergure.

El castillo, que entre tanto ya se encontraba en mal estado, hoy se presenta completamente saneado. Las salas de elaboración de las bodegas han sido también totalmente modernizadas.

Il castello, che per qualche tempo si era trovato in cattive condizioni di conservazione, oggi appare perfettamente restaurato: anche gli impianti di produzione vinicola sono stati modernizzati con grande impiego di risorse.

Château Smith Haut Lafitte

Pessac-Léognan, Bordeaux, France

The foundation of this winery can be traced back to the noble Bosq family about 1365. It owes its current name to Scotsman George Smith, who purchased the estate in the 17th Century in order to export wines to Great Britain. It was, however, Martin Duffour-Dubergier, the mayor of Bordeaux, who established its world fame after he took over the winery estate in 1842. Since 1990, Smith Haut Lafitte has belonged to former skiing pro Daniel Cathiard, who has dedicated himself to carrying on the great tradition through his uncompromising strive for quality.

Die Gründung des Weinguts geht auf die Adelsfamilie der Bosq um 1365 zurück. Seinen heutigen Name verdankt es dem Schotten George Smith, der den Besitz im 17. Jahrhundert erwarb, um die Weine nach England zu exportieren. Doch erst Martin Duffour-Dubergier, Bürgermeister von Bordeaux, der das Weingut ab 1842 führte, begründete dessen Weltruhm. Seit 1990 ist Smith Haut Lafitte im Besitz des ehemaligen Ski-Profis Daniel Cathiard, der sich die Fortsetzung der großen Tradition durch bedingungsloses Qualitätsstreben zur Aufgabe gemacht hat.

La famille noble du Bosq fonda le domaine vers 1365. Toutefois, celui-ci doit son nom actuel à un Ecossais, George Smith, qui l'acheta au 17ème siècle pour en exporter les vins vers l'Angleterre. Puis, c'est seulement Martin Duffour-Dubergier, le maire de Bordeaux, administrateur du domaine à partir de 1842, qui assit sa notoriété internationale. Depuis 1990, Smith Haut Lafitte est entre les mains de l'ancien champion de ski Daniel Cathiard qui s'est donné pour mission de perpétuer une grande tradition dans la recherche permanente de l'excellence.

La fundación de las bodegas se remonta a la familia noble de Bosq, en torno al 1365. El nombre actual se lo debe al escocés George Smith, que adquirió la propiedad en el siglo XVII para transportar los vinos a Inglaterra. Sin embargo sería Martin Duffour-Dubergier, alcalde de Burdeos, quien dirigiera las bodegas a partir de 1842 y les diera su fama mundial. Desde 1990 Smith Haut Lafitte está en manos del antiguo esquiador profesional Daniel Cathiard, quien se ha hecho con la misión de continuar la gran tradición a través de un alto nivel de calidad sin compromisos.

Nonostante sia stata fondata verso 1365 dalla nobile famiglia dei Bosq, la tenuta deve il suo nome odierno allo scozzese George Smith, che nel XVII secolo acquistò la proprietà per esportarne i vini in Inghilterra. Ma solo con Martin Duffour-Dubergier, il sindaco di Bordeaux che subentrò alla guida della tenuta dal 1842, essa assurse a fama mondiale. Dal 1990 Smith Haut Lafitte è proprietà dell'ex campione di sci Daniel Cathiard, il quale si è prefisso di preservarne la grande tradizione, perseguendo con determinazione una politica qualitativa di assoluta eccellenza.

Daniel Cathiard and his wife Florence, owners of Château Smith Haut Lafitte

Daniel Cathiard und seine Frau Florence, Eigentümer von Château Smith Haut Lafitte

Daniel Cathiard et sa femme Florence, propriétaires du Château Smith Haut Lafitte

Daniel Cathiard y su esposa Florence, propietarios de Château Smith Haut Lafitte

Daniel Cathiard con la moglie Florence, proprietari di Château Smith Haut Lafitte

62   Château Smith Haut Lafitte   *Pessac-Léognan, Bordeaux, France*

The winery is situated on a gentle slope with gravel surfaces. The gravel provides the vine roots with optimal irrigation and reflects the sunlight, which encourages optimal maturity of the grapes.

Das Weingut liegt auf einer leichten Anhöhe mit Kiesböden. Der Kies erlaubt den Rebwurzeln eine optimale Wasserversorgung und reflektiert das Sonnenlicht. Dies unterstützt den optimalen Reifeprozess der Trauben.

Le vignoble se situe sur une butte en pente douce, avec un sol couvert de gravier. Le gravier permet une irrigation optimale des pieds de vigne et reflète la lumière du soleil. Ceci favorise le mûrissage optimal des raisins.

Las bodegas están ubicadas sobre una ligera elevación con suelos de guijarro. El guijarro proporciona un abastecimiento de agua óptimo a las raíces de las cepas y refleja la luz solar. Con ello se potencia el proceso de maduración de la uva.

L'azienda vinicola è situata su un lieve rilievo collinare dai terreni ghiaiosi. La ghiaia consente l'ideale apporto d'acqua alle radici dei vitigni e riflette la luce del sole, favorendo così un ottimale processo di maturazione dell'uva.

Under Daniel Cathiard, extensive investments were made in the cellar and production facilities, and the living quarters as well as the representative quarters housed in an 18th Century monastery underwent meticulous renovations.

Unter Daniel Cathiard erfolgten nicht nur umfangreiche Investitionen in die Keller- und Produktionsanlagen, auch die in einer Kartause aus dem 18. Jahrhundert untergebrachten Wohn- und Repräsentationsräume wurden aufwendig renoviert.

Daniel Cathiard a non seulement beaucoup investi dans les installations de production et les caves, mais il a aussi procédé à une coûteuse rénovation des pièces d'habitation et des salles de représentation situées dans une chartreuse du 18ème siècle.

Daniel Cathiard no sólo ha llevado a cabo grandes inversiones en las bodegas y plantas de elaboración sino que además ha renovado en detalle las salas de representación y vivienda ubicadas en la taberna del siglo XVIII.

Sotto la direzione di Daniel Cathiard sono stati fatti non solo importanti investimenti nelle cantine e negli impianti di produzione, ma si è anche effettuato un completo restauro dei locali — alloggiati in una certosa del XVIII secolo — destinati ad abitazione e a scopi di rappresentanza.

Château Canon la Gaffelière

Saint-Emilion, Bordeaux, France

The vineyards of Canon la Gaffelière lie in the Dordogne Valley, along the southern slopes above the village of Saint-Emilion. The winery has been part of the estate of the von Neipperg family since 1971 and has been under the management of Count Stephan von Neipperg since 1985. Owing to the meticulous care of the vines and sophisticated vinification, Canon la Gaffelière has evolved into one of the best Grand Cru Classé wineries under his management, producing between 50,000 and 60,000 bottles of exquisite quality a year.

Die Weinberge von Canon la Gaffelière liegen im Tal der Dordogne, entlang der Südhänge oberhalb des kleinen Ortes Saint-Emilion. Das Weingut befindet sich seit 1971 im Besitz der Familie von Neipperg und wird seit 1985 von Graf Stephan von Neipperg geleitet. Dank sorgfältiger Rebenpflege und anspruchsvoller Vinifikation hat sich Canon la Gaffelière unter seiner Leitung zu einem der besten Grand Cru Classé-Weingüter entwickelt und produziert jährlich ca. 50.000 bis 60.000 Flaschen von ausgesuchter Qualität.

Le vignoble du Château Canon la Gaffelière s'étend dans la vallée de la Dordogne, sur le versant sud des coteaux qui dominent le bourg de Saint-Emilion. Depuis 1971, le domaine est la propriété de la famille von Neipperg et c'est le comte Stephan von Neipperg qui le dirige depuis 1985. Grâce aux soins méticuleux apportés à la vigne et à une vinification exigeante, le Château Canon la Gaffelière est devenu, sous sa conduite, l'un des meilleurs Grands Crus Classés. Le domaine produit chaque année entre 50 000 et 60 000 bouteilles d'une qualité exceptionnelle.

Los viñedos de Canon la Gaffelière están ubicados en el valle de Dordogne, a lo largo de la vertiente sur sobre la pequeña población de Saint-Emilion. Las bodegas son propiedad de la familia von Neipperg desde 1971 y están dirigidas por el conde Stephan von Neipperg desde 1985. Gracias a un esmerado cuidado de las cepas y el exigente proceso de vinificación, Canon la Gaffelière se ha convertido bajo su dirección en una de las mejores bodegas Grand Cru Classé, con una producción anual de unas 50.000 a 60.000 botellas de selecta calidad.

I vigneti di Canon la Gaffelière si trovano nella valle della Dordogne, lungo i declivi meridionali al di sopra della cittadina di Saint-Emilion. Dal 1985 guida la tenuta, che dal 1971 appartiene alla famiglia von Neipperg, il Conte Stephan von Neipperg. Grazie all'attenta cura dei vitigni e ad una vinificazione ricercata, sotto la sua direzione Canon la Gaffelière è divenuta una delle migliori tenute Grand Cru Classé e produce ogni anno tra le 50.000 e le 60.000 bottiglie di qualità scelta.

*Count Stephan von Neipperg, owner of
Château Canon la Gaffelière, with his family*

*Graf Stephan von Neipperg, Eigentümer von
Château Canon la Gaffelière, mit seiner Familie*

*Comte Stephan von Neipperg, propriétaire du
Château Canon la Gaffelière avec sa famille*

*Conde Stephan von Neipperg, propietario de
Château Canon la Gaffelière junto a su familia*

*Conte Stephan von Neipperg, proprietario di
Château Canon la Gaffelière, con la sua famiglia*

Some of the remarkable quarters of this winery are available for wine tasting—based on appointment. A particularly awe-inspiring sight is the reception room, where you can find the register with some illustrious names in it.

Ein Teil der beeindruckenden Räume des Weingutes stehen — nach vorheriger Vereinbarung — für Degustationen zur Verfügung. Besonders beeindruckend ist das Kaminzimmer, in dem auch das Gästebuch mit illustren Eintragungen liegt.

Une partie des remarquables pièces du domaine est à la disposition des visiteurs — sur réservation préalable — pour des dégustations. La pièce à la cheminée, dans laquelle est placé le livre d'or contenant d'illustres signatures, est particulièrement impressionnante.

Parte de las impresionantes salas de las bodegas se ponen a disposición para catas, bajo previo acuerdo. El salón con chimenea resulta especialmente fascinante; allí reposa un libro de visitas que contiene las anotaciones de personajes ilustres.

Una parte degli splendidi locali della tenuta è a disposizione per degustazioni su appuntamento. Colpisce in particolare la sala del camino in cui si trova anche il libro degli ospiti, dove compaiono nomi di illustri visitatori.

Château Canon la Gaffelière   *Saint-Emilion, Bordeaux, France*   69

Château Figeac

Saint-Emilion, Bordeaux, France

A certain Figeacus established a villa as early as the 2nd Century A. C. where the present estate is now located—traces of the antique irrigation system can be found there to this day. In the 17th Century, the estate went to the Carle family, which expanded it into 618 acres, until it broke up due to numerous changes in ownership and partitions in the 19th Century. In 1896, André Villepigue, the great grandfather of the present owner, acquired the present estate. A particularly remarkable sight is the main façade of the Château, whose proportions are based on the golden section.

Ein gewisser Figeacus errichtete schon im 2. Jahrhundert nach Christus eine Villa an der Stelle des heutigen Guts – bis heute finden sich hier Spuren des antiken Bewässerungssystems. Im 17. Jahrhundert fiel das Gut an die Familie Carle, die es zu einem 250 ha großen Besitz erweiterte, der im 19. Jahrhundert durch zahlreiche Besitzerwechsel und Teilungen zerfiel. 1896 erwarb André Villepigue, der Urgroßvater des jetzigen Eigentümers, das heutige Gut. Besonders eindrucksvoll ist die Hauptfassade des Châteaus, deren Proportionen auf dem goldenen Schnitt beruhen.

Un certain Figeacus érigea, dès le 2ème siècle après J.-C., une villa sur l'emplacement du domaine actuel – aujourd'hui encore, on trouve des traces de l'ancien système d'irrigation. Au 17ème siècle, le domaine devint la propriété de la famille Carle qui étendit sa surface à 250 hectares. Mais il se désagrégea au 19ème siècle en raison de nombreux changements de propriétaires et de partages. André Villepigue, l'arrière-grand-père de l'actuel propriétaire, en fit l'acquisition en 1896. La façade principale du château est particulièrement impressionnante, car ses proportions se basent sur la section d'or.

Ya en el siglo II d.C., un tal Figeacus construyó una mansión en el lugar donde se encuentra actualmente la propiedad. Y aún hoy existen huellas del antiguo sistema de irrigación. En el siglo XVII el dominio pasó a la familia Carle, quien lo amplió hasta convertirlo en una propiedad de 250 hectáreas, que durante el siglo XIX pasaría por numerosos propietarios y particiones. En 1896 adquirió la bodega que es hoy André Villepigue, el bisabuelo del actual propietario. Impresiona la fachada principal del Château, que mantiene claramente la "divina proporción".

Già nel II secolo dopo Cristo un certo Figeacus costruì nel luogo dove oggi si trova la tenuta una villa romana, come dimostrano le tracce dell'antico sistema d'irrigazione conservatesi fino ad oggi. Nel XVII secolo la tenuta passò nelle mani della famiglia Carle, che ne ampliò l'estensione fino a raggiungere i 250 ettari. Dopo una fase di decadenza dovuta a vari cambi di proprietà e spartizioni avvenuti nel corso del XIX secolo, nel 1896 la tenuta nella sua veste attuale fu acquistata da André Villepigue, il bisnonno dell'attuale proprietario. Di particolare rilievo la facciata principale del castello, progettata seguendo le proporzioni della sezione aurea.

Thierry Manoncourt, owner
of *Château Figeac*

Thierry Manoncourt, Eigentümer
von *Château Figeac*

Thierry Manoncourt, propriétaire
du *Château Figeac*

Thierry Manoncourt, propietario
de *Château Figeac*

Thierry Manoncourt, proprietario
di *Château Figeac*

CHATEAU-FIGEAC
PREMIER GRAND CRU CLASSÉ
St ÉMILION
2004
Bouteille № 106608

After the Château Figeac *was among the pioneers in the use of stainless steel tanks in the 1960s, fermentation is once again done with oak tubs today.*

Nachdem das Château Figeac *in den 60er-Jahren zu den Pionieren im Einsatz von Edelstahltanks gehörte, findet die Gärung heute wieder in Eichenbottichen statt.*

Dans les années 60, *le Château Figeac avait été le pionnier de l'emploi des cuves en inox ; aujourd'hui la fermentation se fait de nouveau dans des barriques de chêne.*

Después de que el Château Figeac *se convirtiera en los años 60 en el pionero en el empleo de depósitos de acero inoxidable, hoy la fermentación se vuelve a llevar a cabo en tinas de roble.*

Nonostante negli anni Sessanta Château Figeac *sia stato uno dei pionieri dell'utilizzo di serbatoi in acciaio inox, oggi si è tornati a far fermentare il vino in tini di rovere.*

The richly furnished, elegant interior of the castle makes it seem like time is at a standstill.

In den reich ausgestatteten, stilvollen Innenräumen des Schlosses scheint die Zeit still zu stehen.

Dans les intérieurs du château, pleins de style et richement garnis, le temps semble s'être arrêté.

En los ricamente decorados interiores cargados de estilo, parece haberse parado el tiempo.

Negli interni del castello, arredati riccamente e con gusto, il tempo pare essersi fermato.

Château Pavie

Saint-Emilion, Bordeaux, France

This winery was established in the late 19th Century when wine merchant Ferdinand Bouffard bought a whole range of smaller estates and combined them into a new winery estate, which he named Pavie, or "vineyard peach". Thus evolved the largest Premier Grand Cru Classé estate in Saint-Emilion. In the 20th Century, Château Pavie changed ownership several times. Since 1998, it has been under the ownership of Gérard Perse, a businessman, who had wide-ranging renovation measures carried out and has been very successful at managing the winery ever since.

Das Gut entstand Ende des 19. Jahrhunderts, als der Weinhändler Ferdinand Bouffard eine ganze Reihe kleinerer Besitzungen kaufte und zu einem neuen Weingut zusammenfasste, dem er den Namen Pavie, Weinbergspfirsich, gab. So entstand die größte Premier Grand Cru Classé-Besitzung in Saint-Emilion. Im 20. Jahrhundert wechselte Château Pavie mehrfach den Eigentümer. Seit 1998 ist es im Besitz von Gérard Perse, einem Geschäftsmann, der umfangreiche Modernisierungsmaßnahmen durchführen ließ und das Weingut seither mit großem Erfolg führt.

Le domaine se créa à la fin du 19ème siècle, quand le négociant en vins Ferdinand Bouffard se porta acquéreur d'une série de petites parcelles qu'il réunit en un grand domaine, auquel il attribua le nom de « Pavie », pêche de vigne. C'est ainsi que se constitua le plus grand vignoble Premier Grand Cru Classé à Saint-Emilion. Au 20ème siècle, le Château Pavie changea plusieurs fois de propriétaire. Depuis 1998, il appartient à Gérard Perse, un homme d'affaires qui entreprit une modernisation de grande envergure et qui, depuis lors, dirige le domaine avec le plus grand succès.

El dominio surgió a finales del siglo XIX, cuando el bodeguero Ferdinand Bouffard compró una serie de propiedades para hacer de ellas un dominio de viñedos al que dio el nombre Pavie, pavía. De ahí nacieron las mayores propiedades Grand Cru Classé en Saint-Emilion. Durante el siglo XX Château Pavie cambió de dueño en numerosas ocasiones. Desde 1998 pertenece a Gérard Perse, un hombre de negocios que llevando a cabo amplias medidas de modernización dotó a las bodegas del éxito que portan desde entonces.

La tenuta nacque verso la fine del XIX secolo, quando il commerciante di vini Ferdinand Bouffard acquistò tutta una serie di piccoli possedimenti accorpandoli in una nuova azienda vinicola cui diede il nome di Pavie, che in italiano significa "pesca del vignaiolo". Fu così che nacque il più grande possedimento Premier Grand Cru Classé a Saint-Emilion. Dopo essere passato di mano varie volte nel corso del XX secolo, Château Pavie dal 1998 è proprietà di Gérard Perse, un uomo d'affari che da allora, dopo aver effettuato notevoli interventi di modernizzazione, guida la tenuta con grande successo.

Gérard Perse, owner of Château Pavie, with his family

Gérard Perse, Eigentümer von Château Pavie, mit seiner Familie

Gérard Perse, propriétaire du Château Pavie, avec sa famille

Gerard Perse, propietario de Château Pavie junto a su familia

Gerard Perse, proprietario di Château Pavie, con la sua famiglia

The Château is located to the southeast of the Appellation Saint-Emilion, roughly a mile from the community of Saint-Emilion. Due to excessive moisture and cold, the old cellars, which are partially situated in the vineyards, have been replaced with new modern facilities by now.

Das Château liegt im Südosten der Appellation Saint-Emilion, rund 1,5 km von der Gemeinde Saint-Emilion entfernt. Die alten, zum Teil in den Weinbergen gelegen Keller wurden aufgrund zu großer Feuchtigkeit und Kälte inzwischen durch moderne Neubauten ersetzt.

Le château se trouve au sud-est de l'appellation Saint-Emilion, à environ 1,5 km du village de Saint-Emilion. Les anciennes caves, situées pour certaines dans les vignes, trop humides et trop froides, ont été entretemps remplacées par des bâtiments neufs modernes.

El Château está ubicado al sureste de la apelación de Saint-Emilion, a unos 1,5 km del municipio de Saint-Emilion. A causa de la enorme humedad y el frío, las antiguas bodegas, algunas de ellas levantadas entre los viñedos, han sido sustituidas progresivamente por nuevos y modernos edificios.

Château Pavie è situato nella zona sud-orientale dell'Appellation Saint-Emilion, a circa un chilometro e mezzo di distanza dall'omonima cittadina. Le vecchie cantine, in parte scavate nelle colline, a causa dell'eccessiva umidità e della temperatura troppo bassa sono state sostituite da moderni edifici di nuova costruzione.

Domaine de la Pousse d'Or

Côte d'Or, Burgundy, France

Jean-Nicolas Ferté and Gérard Potel founded this winery in its present form in 1964. This was after the Clos de la Bousse d'Or and other vineyards that used to belong to the 247-acre estate of Duvault-Blochet in the late 19th Century had been divided into various parts and sold. Following Potel's death, the winery was acquired by Patrick Landanger in 1997, who has since then continuously expanded the top position of the domain among the estates of Burgundy. Most of the present estate dates back to the time of Napoleon I and rests on vaults that date back to the 13th Century.

Das Weingut in seiner heutigen Form wurde 1964 von Jean-Nicolas Ferté und Gérard Potel gegründet, nachdem der Clos de la Bousse d'Or und andere Lagen, die Ende des 19. Jahrhunderts zu dem 100 ha großen Gut Duvault-Blochet gehört hatten, zuvor verschiedentlich geteilt und verkauft worden waren. Nach dem Tode von Potel wurde das Weingut 1997 von Patrick Landanger übernommen, der die Spitzenposition der Domäne unter den Gütern des Burgunds seither weiter ausbaute. Das heutige Gutshaus stammt größtenteils aus der Zeit Napoleons I. und ruht auf Kellergewölben, die in das 13. Jahrhundert datieren.

Le domaine tel qu'il existe aujourd'hui fut créé en 1964 par Jean-Nicolas Ferté et Gérard Potel, après que le Clos de la Bousse d'Or et d'autres parcelles ayant fait partie, à la fin du 19ème siècle, des 100 hectares du domaine Duvault-Blochet, eurent été diversement partagés et vendus. A la mort de Potel, le domaine fut repris en 1997 par Patrick Landanger qui, depuis lors, a encore consolidé la place de premier plan qu'il occupe parmi les domaines viticoles de Bourgogne. La plus grande partie de l'actuel manoir date de l'époque de Napoléon Ier et s'appuie sur des caves voûtées datant du 13ème siècle.

Las bodegas en su estado actual fueron fundadas por Jean-Nicolas Ferté y Gérard Potel en 1964, después de que el Clos de la Bousse d'Or y otras ubicaciones que a finales del siglo XIX pertenecían a la propiedad Duvault-Blochet, de 100 hectáreas, fueran divididas en diversas formas y vendidas posteriormente. Tras la muerte de Potel en 1997 adquirió las bodegas Patrick Landanger, que desde ese momento comenzó a potenciar la posición privilegiada que tiene hoy el dominio entre las propiedades de Borgoña. La casa señorial actual se remonta a la época de Napoleón I y se levanta sobre un abovedado subterráneo del siglo XIII.

La tenuta come la vediamo oggi nasce nel 1964 per iniziativa di Jean-Nicolas Ferté e Gérard Potel, in seguito alla vendita e alle molteplici spartizioni di Clos de la Bousse d'Or e di altri vigneti, che sul finire del XIX secolo avevano fatto parte dei 100 ettari di tenuta di Duvault-Blochet. Nel 1997, dopo la morte di Potel, gli è subentrato nella guida della tenuta Patrick Landanger, che da allora ne ha ulteriormente sviluppato la posizione di punta tra le aziende vinicole della Borgogna. L'odierno palazzo risale in gran parte all'epoca di Napoleone I e poggia su cantine con soffitto a volta datate al XIII secolo.

Patrick Landanger, owner of
Domaine de la Pousse d'Or

Patrick Landanger, Eigentümer der
Domaine de la Pousse d'Or

Patrick Landanger, propriétaire du
Domaine de la Pousse d'Or

Patrick Landanger, propietario de
Domaine de la Pousse d'Or

Patrick Landanger, proprietario di
Domaine de la Pousse d'Or

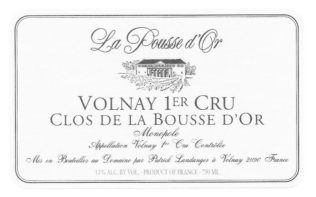

The landscape of Burgundy *resembles a gigantic quilt of small vineyards often surrounded by low stone walls.*

Die Landschaft Burgunds *gleicht einem riesigen Flickenteppich aus kleinen Weinbergslagen, die häufig von niedrigen Steinmauern umgeben sind.*

Les paysages bourguignons *ressemblent à une mosaïque de petites parcelles de vignes souvent entourées de bas murets de pierre.*

El paisaje de Borgoña *semeja a una alfombra remendada de pequeños viñedos, algunos enmarcados por muros de piedra de poca altura.*

Il paesaggio della Borgogna *somiglia ad un enorme patchwork di piccoli vigneti, spesso delimitati da bassi muretti di pietra.*

La Pousse d'Or
POMMARD
LES JAROLLIERES
La Pousse d'Or
POMMARD

The solid, wooden-paneled degustation room of the winery estate offers the right environment for tasting the exclusive wines, which are only produced in Premier or Grand Cru quality.

Der gediegene, holzvertäfelte Degustationsraum des Weingutes bietet das passende Umfeld für den Genuss der exklusiven Weine, die nur in Premier oder Grand Cru Qualität produziert werden.

La salle de dégustation élégante, aux lambris boisés, constitue un cadre idéal pour savourer les vins exclusifs, uniquement des Premiers Crus ou des Grands Crus.

La sala de catas de la bodega, revestida de madera, ofrece el ambiente adecuado para poder disfrutar de vinos exclusivos, que aquí se producen sólo al nivel de calidad Premier o Grand Cru.

La sala di degustazione della tenuta, in stile tradizionale e con le pareti rivestite in legno, è senz'altro la cornice ideale per degustare gli esclusivi vini, prodotti solo in qualità Premier o Grand Cru.

Louis Latour

Côte d'Or, Burgundy, France

The foundation of this winery can be traced back to Jean Latour, who began growing grapevine in the region of Aloxe-Corton in 1768. Succeeding generations have continuously expanded the estate, which remains family-owned to this day. By now, the Louis Latour winery estate includes at least 125 acres of vineyards along with the largest property of Grand Cru vineyards along the Côte d'Or, at 71 acres. The Château on the edge of Aloxe-Corton was built in 1742. The production site dates back to the year 1832 and is considered one of the oldest, still operating wine cellars in France.

Die Gründung des Weingutes geht auf Jean Latour zurück, der seit 1768 im Gebiet von Aloxe-Corton Rebstöcke angepflanzt hatte. Von den nachfolgenden Generationen wurde das Gut, das sich bis heute in Familienbesitz befindet, beständig erweitert. Inzwischen gehören zum Weingut Louis Latour gut 50 ha Rebflächen, darunter der mit 28 ha größte Besitz von Grand Cru-Lagen an der Côte d'Or. Das Château am Rande von Aloxe-Corton wurde 1742 errichtet. Das Produktionsgebäude stammt aus dem Jahre 1832 und gilt als eine der ältesten noch in Betrieb befindlichen Kellereien Frankreichs.

La fondation du domaine remonte à Jean Latour qui planta des vignes dès 1768 dans la région d'Aloxe-Corton. Le domaine, qui reste aujourd'hui encore une propriété familiale, n'a cessé de s'agrandir sous l'impulsion des générations suivantes. Entre-temps, le domaine Louis Latour compte au moins 50 hectares de vignes, parmi lesquelles la plus grande propriété – 28 hectares – des Grands Crus de la Côte d'Or. Le château, situé aux abords d'Aloxe-Corton, fut construit en 1742. La cuverie date de 1832 et représente l'un des plus anciens bâtiments de ce type encore en fonctionnement aujourd'hui en France.

La fundación de las bodegas se remite a Jean Latour, quien ya desde 1768 plantaba cepas en la zona de Aloxe-Corton. A partir de las generaciones posteriores la propiedad fue ampliada constantemente. Entre tanto a las bodegas Louis Latour pertenecen 50 hectáreas de viñedo, entre ellas la mayor propiedad, 28 hectáreas, de Grand Cru viñas en la Côte d'Or. El Château, ubicado en los límites de Aloxe-Corton, fue construido en 1742. El edificio de producción se remonta al año 1832 y se considera una de las bodegas más antiguas en funcionamiento de Francia.

La storia della tenuta inizia con Jean Latour, che sin dal 1768 aveva cominciato a piantare vitigni nell'area di Aloxe-Corton. Le generazioni seguenti provvidero ad ampliare costantemente la tenuta, che da allora è rimasta proprietà della famiglia. Oggi la tenuta Louis Latour comprende ben 50 ettari di vigneti, tra cui, con i suoi 28 ettari, la più grande estensione di vigne Grand Cru sulla Côte d'Or. Il castello, situato ai margini del territorio cittadino di Aloxe-Corton, fu costruito nel 1742, mentre l'edificio destinato alla vinificazione risale al 1832 ed è considerato una delle più antiche cantine vinicole ancora funzionanti in Francia.

Louis-Fabrice Latour (CEO), the family's seventh Louis Latour to run Maison Louis Latour

Louis-Fabrice Latour (CEO), der siebte Louis Latour, der das gleichnamige Weingut führt

Louis-Fabrice Latour (PDG), le septième Louis Latour qui dirige le domaine du même nom

Louis-Fabrice Latour (CEO), el séptimo Louis Latour, que dirige las bodegas del mismo nombre

Louis-Fabrice Latour (CEO), il settimo Louis Latour alla guida dell'omonima azienda vinicola

GRAND VIN DE BOURGOGNE

Château

1749

Corton Grancey

GRAND CRU

APPELLATION CORTON CONTRÔLÉE

MIS EN BOUTEILLE A BEAUNE PAR LOUIS LATOUR NÉGOCIANT-ÉLEVEUR

LOUIS LATOUR A BEAUNE - CÔTE-D'OR - FRANCE

The first single-function building *of its kind in France, the cellar consists of three levels, two of which are situated underground. Here the grapes are transported in large open copper vats by means of a rail system.*

Die Kelleranlage, der erste Zweckbau dieser Art *in Frankreich, besteht aus drei Geschossen, von denen zwei unterirdisch liegen. Die Trauben werden hier mit Hilfe eines Schienensystems in großen, offenen Kupferkesseln transportiert.*

La cave, le premier bâtiment fonctionnel de ce type *en France, est construite sur trois étages, dont deux souterrains. Ici, les raisins sont transportés, au moyen d'un système de rail, dans de grandes cuves de cuivre ouvertes.*

Las instalaciones de las bodegas, *primera construcción funcional de este tipo existente en Francia, se componen de tres plantas, de las cuales dos son subterráneas. Las uvas se transportan en grandes calderas abiertas de cobre por medio de un sistema de carriles.*

L'edificio che ospita le cantine, *il primo di questo genere in Francia, dispone di tre piani, di cui due sotterranei. L'uva viene trasportata in grandi recipienti di rame aperti grazie ad un sistema su rotaie.*

Marqués de Riscal

Rioja, Spain

Founded in 1858, the Marqués de Riscal winery in Elciego is the oldest still existing bodega in the Rioja region. Ever since, the estate has earned a reputation for being highly innovative. The winery's latest coup is the recently completed "Ciudad del Vino." This complex, which houses a hotel, a spa with vino-therapy, a restaurant, a conference center and a wine museum, includes both the historic bodega and the eye-catching new design by American star architect Frank O. Gehry.

Das Weingut Marqués de Riscal in Elciego wurde 1858 gegründet und ist damit die älteste noch bestehende Bodega im Rioja-Gebiet. Seit jeher gilt das Gut als besonders innovationsfreudig. Der aktuellste Coup des Weingutes ist die gerade fertiggestellte „Ciudad del Vino". Zu dem Komplex, in dem sich ein Hotel, ein Spa mit Vinotherapie, ein Restaurant, ein Kongresszentrum und ein Weinmuseum befinden, gehören sowohl die historische Bodega als auch der aufsehenerregende Neubau des amerikanischen Stararchitekten Frank O. Gehry.

Le domaine Marqués de Riscal à Elciego fut fondé en 1858 ; c'est ainsi la cave la plus ancienne existant encore dans la région de la Rioja. Depuis toujours, le domaine passe pour être particulièrement ouvert à l'innovation. Le dernier coup de maître du domaine est la « Ciudad del Vino » (Cité du Vin) dont la construction vient de s'achever. Le complexe qui présente un hôtel, un spa avec centre de vinothérapie, un restaurant, des salles de conférences et un musée du vin, comprend la cave historique ainsi que le nouveau bâtiment extravagant, réalisé par la star de l'architecture américaine Frank O. Gehry.

Las bodegas de Marqués de Riscal en Elciego fueron fundadas en 1858 y se trata de las más antiguas ubicadas en la zona de La Rioja. A las bodegas se las conoce desde siempre por su carácter innovador. Actualmente el máximo atractivo de la propiedad es la "Ciudad del Vino". El complejo cuenta con hotel, spa de vinoterapia, restaurante, centro de conferencias, un museo del vino y a él pertenecen también tanto la bodega histórica como una imponente nueva construcción, obra del famoso arquitecto americano Frank O. Gehry.

La tenuta Marqués de Riscal fu fondata a Elciego nel 1858 ed è quindi la più antica Bodega ancora in funzione nella regione del Rioja. Da sempre è considerata un'azienda vinicola particolarmente attenta all'innovazione. L'ultimo colpo messo a segno dalla tenuta è la "Ciudad del vino", di recente realizzazione: del complesso, in cui si trovano un albergo, un centro benessere specializzato in vinoterapia, un ristorante, un centro congressi e un museo enologico, fanno parte tanto l'antica Bodega quanto il nuovo, spettacolare edificio progettato dal celebre architetto americano Frank O. Gehry.

Don Camilo Hurtado de Amézaga,
the first Margrave of Riscal and original owner of the winery

Don Camilo Hurtado de Amézaga,
der erste Markgraf von Riscal und ursprüngliche Besitzer des Weingutes

Don Camilo Hurtado de Amézaga,
le premier marquis de Riscal et propriétaire d'origine du domaine

Don Camilo Hurtado de Amézaga,
primer marqués de Riscal y propietario original de las bodegas

Don Camilo Hurtado de Amézaga,
il primo marchese di Riscal, primo proprietario della tenuta

The spectacular new design of the "Ciudad del Vino" with its seemingly chaotic structure and striking titanium roof has helped this winery estate captivate the attention of the international press.

Der spektakuläre Neubau der „Ciudad del Vino" mit seiner scheinbar chaotischen Struktur und dem auffälligen Titandach sicherte dem Weingut die Aufmerksamkeit der internationalen Presse.

Le spectaculaire complexe de la « Cité du Vin » avec sa structure apparemment chaotique et son toit en titane impressionnant a vu converger sur lui les regards de la presse internationale.

La espectacular construcción de la "Ciudad del Vino" con su aparentemente caótica estructura y el llamativo tejado de titanio convirtió a la propiedad en centro de atención de la prensa internacional.

Lo spettacolare nuovo complesso della "Ciudad del Vino", con la sua struttura apparentemente caotica e l'appariscente tetto in titanio ha assicurato alla tenuta l'attenzione della stampa internazionale.

Ysios

Rioja, Spain

The silhouette of stacked wine barrels inspired Spanish architect Santiago Calatrava for his spectacular design for the Ysios winery. Located at the foot of the Sierra Cantabria, this expressive structure perfectly blends into the landscape of the Rioja Alavesa. Another one of its unique aspects is the ceremonious, almost sacral character of the production, warehousing and degustation facilities inside the building. It is a place where avant-garde architecture meets the deliberately traditional production techniques of Ysios.

Die Silhouette gestapelter Weinfässer inspirierte den spanischen Architekten Santiago Calatrava zu seinem spektakulären Entwurf für das Weingut Ysios. Am Fuße der Sierra Cantabria gelegen, fügt sich der expressive Bau perfekt in die Landschaft des Rioja Alavesa ein. Außergewöhnlich ist auch der feierliche, beinahe sakrale Charakter der Produktions-, Lager- und Degustationsräume im Inneren des Gebäudes. Im Gegensatz zu der avantgardistischen Architektur stehen die bewusst traditionellen Produktionsmethoden von Ysios.

C'est la silhouette de fûts empilés qui inspira à l'architecte espagñol Santiago Calatrava son projet spectaculaire pour le domaine d'Ysios. Au pied des monts Cantabriques, cette étrange bodega s'intègre parfaitement dans le paysage de la Rioja Alavesa. A l'intérieur du bâtiment, les salles de dégustation et de production et le chai, aux allures de cathédrale, constituent un univers où le dieu « vin » règne en maître. Les méthodes de production d'Ysios, délibérément traditionnelles, contrastent avec l'architecture avant-gardiste.

La silueta que forman las hileras de barricas sirvió de inspiración al arquitecto español Santiago Calatrava para crear el espectacular boceto para las bodegas Ysios. La expresiva construcción se ubica a los pies de la Sierra de Cantabria, fundiéndose a la perfección con el paisaje de la Rioja Alavesa. También resultan fuera de lo común los espacios de producción, almacenamiento y degustación, de carácter festivo, casi incluso sagrado, ubicados en el interior del edifico. Pero al contrario que su vanguardista arquitectura, los métodos de producción de las bodegas Ysios permanecen fieles a los métodos de producción tradicionales.

Il profilo dei fusti di vino accatastati ha ispirato all'architetto spagnolo Santiago Calatrava il suo spettacolare progetto per l'azienda vinicola Ysios. Situato ai piedi della Sierra Cantabria, l'edificio s'inserisce perfettamente con la sua espressività nel paesaggio del Rioja Alavesa. Straordinario è anche il carattere solenne, quasi sacrale dei locali destinati alla produzione, all'invecchiamento e alla degustazione del vino, situati nel cuore dell'edificio. Il fatto che Ysios abbia consapevolmente scelto di applicare metodi di vinificazione tradizionali fa da interessante contrappunto a questa architettura avanguardistica.

Juan Antonio Mompó,
General Director of Domecq Bodegas

Juan Antonio Mompó,
Generaldirektor der Domecq Bodegas

Juan Antonio Mompó,
Directeur Général des Bodegas Domecq

Juan Antonio Mompó,
director general de las bodegas Domecq

Juan Antonio Mompó,
direttore generale di Domecq Bodegas

The soft up and down of the roof landscape of Ysios also characterizes the interior of the building. The centrally located tasting room offers a wide-ranging view of the vineyards of the estate.

Das sanfte Auf und Ab der Dachlandschaft von Ysios prägt auch die Innenräume des Gebäudes. Von dem zentral angeordneten Probierraum aus hat man einen weiten Blick über die Rebflächen des Weingutes.

Le toit de la bodega d'Ysios ondule légèrement comme le paysage alentour et ce mouvement se retrouve dans les salles du bâtiment. La salle de dégustation en est le centre et offre une vue panoramique sur les vignes du domaine.

Los suaves altibajos en el paisaje de tejados de Ysios caracterizan también los interiores del edificio. Desde la sala de catas, situada en el centro, se abren las vistas a los vastos viñedos de estas bodegas.

Il dolce moto ondulato che caratterizza il tetto di Ysios si rispecchia anche all'interno dell'edificio. Dalla sala di degustazione, che occupa una posizione centrale, si gode un'ampia vista sui vigneti della tenuta.

Enate

Aragon, Spain

Founded in 1991, this winery is located in the province of Huesca, at the narrowest point of the Iberian Peninsula. Here, in the region of Somontano at the foot of the Pyrenees, Atlantic and Mediterranean weather influences collide to form a unique climate. Enate defines itself as an ultramodern "21st Century winery estate," an aspiration also expressed in the estate's cool, yet elegant and stylish architecture. Enate owes its fame in no small part to its special labels, which are designed by such influential Spanish artists as Antoni Tàpies or Eduardo Chillida.

Das 1991 gegründete Weingut liegt in der Provinz Huesca, an der schmalsten Stelle der spanischen Halbinsel. Hier, in der Region Somontano am Fuße der Pyrenäen, treffen atlantische und mediterrane Wettereinflüsse aufeinander und schaffen ein einzigartiges Klima. Enate definiert sich als hochmodernes „Weingut des 21. Jahrhunderts", ein Anspruch, der auch in der kühlen, gleichwohl eleganten und stilvollen Architektur des Gutes seinen Ausdruck findet. Berühmt ist Enate nicht zuletzt für seine besonderen Etiketten, die von bedeutenden spanischen Künstlern wie Antoni Tàpies oder Eduardo Chillida gestaltet werden.

Le domaine, fondé en 1991, se situe dans la province de Huesca, soit la partie la plus étroite de la péninsule ibérique. Cette région de Somontano, au pied des Pyrénées, au croisement des diverses influences du temps venant de l'Atlantique et de la Méditerranée, bénéficie d'un climat unique. Enate se définit comme un « domaine ultramoderne du 21ème siècle », une exigence que traduit bien l'architecture froide, bien qu'élégante et stylisée du domaine. Enfin, Enate est également célèbre pour ses étiquettes spéciales, dessinées par des artistes espagnols de renom comme Antoni Tàpies et Eduardo Chillida.

Las bodegas fundadas en 1991 se encuentran en la provincia de Huesca, en la zona más estrecha de la Península Ibérica. Aquí, en la región Somontano a los pies de los Pirineos, las influencias meteorológicas del Atlántico y el Mediterráneo se aúnan creando un clima singular. Enate se define como "bodega del siglo XXI" con la más moderna tecnología, una imagen visible en su arquitectura fría, elegante y dotada de estilo. Enate es también famosa por sus especiales etiquetas, diseñadas por artistas españoles como Antoni Tàpies o Eduardo Chillida.

La tenuta vinicola, fondata nel 1991, si trova nella provincia di Huesca, nel punto più stretto della penisola spagnola: qui, nella regione di Somontano, ai piedi dei Pirenei, influssi atlantici e mediterranei s'incontrano creando una situazione climatica unica nel suo genere. Enate si autodefinisce una modernissima "azienda vinicola del XXI secolo", e questa ambizione si riflette anche nell'architettura della tenuta, al contempo fredda ed elegante nonché di gran stile. La notorietà dell'azienda poggia non da ultimo sulle particolari etichette delle sue bottiglie, disegnate da noti artisti spagnoli come Antoni Tàpies o Eduardo Chillida.

Wine labels *designed by Antonio Saura (left) and José Beulas (right).*

Weinetikette, *gestaltet von Antonio Saura (links) und José Beulas (rechts).*

Etiquettes de bouteilles *dessinées par Antonio Saura (à gauche) et José Beulas (à droite).*

Etiquetas de vino *diseñadas por Antonio Saura (izquierda) y José Beulas (derecha).*

Etichetta de vino *creata da Antonio Saura (a sinistra) e José Beulas (a destra).*

From the outside, Enate seems like a rather unspectacular, if diligently planned industrial site.

Von außen präsentiert sich Enate als eher unspektakuläre, gleichwohl sorgfältig geplante Industrieanlage.

Vu de l'extérieur, Enate se présente comme un site industriel plutôt ordinaire mais néanmoins minutieusement conçu.

Desde el exterior, Enate aparece como una instalación industrial cuidadosamente planificada pero más bien poco espectacular.

Vista da fuori, Enate si presenta più come un impianto industriale poco spettacolare, per quanto ben pianificato.

In its interior, however, the plain functionality of the rooms is exacerbated by means of highly effective décor.

Im Inneren wird die schlichte Funktionalität der Räume jedoch durch effektvolle Rauminszenierungen überhöht.

A l'intérieur, la fonctionnalité très sobre des espaces est pourtant soulignée par une mise en scène très expressive.

Sin embargo, en los interiores se realza la austera funcionalidad de las estancias a través de disposiciones de los espacios cargadas de efecto.

All'interno però la sobria funzionalità degli spazi viene sublimata da un'efficace messa in scena architettonica.

Señorío de Otazu
Navarra, Spain

Somewhere between tradition and innovation, you'll find the Señorío de Otazu winery, located in the far north of the Navarra region. A few years ago, its medieval castle structure and historic cellar were complemented with new production facilities as well as a state-of-the-art wine warehouse measuring 38,750 square feet. The latter is made of nine concrete vaults, whose elegant arches and clever lighting make it seem more like a cathedral.

Zwischen Tradition und Innovation steht das Weingut Señorío de Otazu, das ganz im Norden des Navarra-Gebietes liegt. Ergänzend zu einer mittelalterlichen Schlossanlage und der historischen Kellerei entstanden vor wenigen Jahren neue Produktionsgebäude sowie ein hochmoderner, 3.600 m² großer Fasskeller. Dieser setzt sich aus neun Betongewölben zusammen, die mit ihrem eleganten Schwung und einer raffinierten Lichtführung einen kathedralenartigen Raumeindruck erzeugen.

Entre tradition et innovation, le domaine d'Señorío de Otazu s'étend tout au nord des terres de la Navarre. Pour compléter le château du Moyen Âge et la cave historique, on construisit, il y a quelques années, de nouvelles installations de production ainsi qu'une immense cave à barriques ultramoderne de 3600 m². Elle est constituée de neuf voûtes en béton auxquelles une architecture élancée et élégante et un éclairage raffiné confèrent des allures de cathédrale.

Las bodegas Señorío de Otazu, ubicadas en el extremo norte de Navarra, oscilan entre la innovación y la tradición. Hace unos años, al castillo medieval y la bodega histórica se añadieron nuevos edificios de producción y una sala de barricas de alta tecnología con 3.600 m². El espacio consiste en nueve bóvedas de hormigón que gracias a su elegante curvatura crean un refinado entramado que difumina la luz al igual que en una catedral.

A mezzo tra tradizione e innovazione si colloca la tenuta di Señorío de Otazu, situata nell'estremo nord della Navarra. Pochi anni fa, a integrare un castello medievale e la storica cantina vinicola, sono sorti nuovi fabbricati per la vinificazione e una modernissima cantina per la conservazione dei fusti, su una superficie di ben 3600 m². Quest'ultima è composta di nove ambienti con soffitto a volta in cemento, i quali grazie al loro elegante slancio e alla raffinata illuminazione ricreano l'atmosfera spaziale di una cattedrale.

Javier Bañales, General Manager of Señorío de Otazu

Javier Bañales, Geschäftsführer von Señorío de Otazu

Javier Bañales, Directeur Général de Señorío de Otazu

Javier Bañales, director gerente de Señorío de Otazu

Javier Bañales, amministratore delegato di Señorío de Otazu

Señorío de Otazu   *Navarra, Spain*   107

Old and new building structures form a harmonious fusion at the Señorío de Otazu winery estate. A particularly remarkable feature is the new wine warehouse with nine concrete vaults ensuring constantly low temperatures throughout the year.

Alte und neue Gebäudeteile verbinden sich im Weingut Señorío de Otazu auf harmonische Weise. Besonders eindrucksvoll ist der neue Fasskeller mit neun Betongewölben, die ganzjährig konstant niedrige Temperaturen sicherstellen.

Le domaine de Señorío de Otazu parvient à une association harmonieuse des bâtiments anciens et des constructions récentes. La nouvelle cave à barriques avec ses neuf voûtes en béton qui garantit des températures basses toute l'année est particulièrement impressionnante.

En las bodegas Señorío de Otazu los sectores nuevos y antiguos del edificio se funden de forma armoniosa. La nueva sala de barricas con sus nueve bóvedas de hormigón mantiene bajas temperaturas constantes durante todo el año.

Nella tenuta di Señorío de Otazu convivono in armonia unità architettoniche nuove e antiche. Colpisce particolarmente la nuova cantina di stoccaggio delle botti, dotata di nove sale coperte da volte in cemento, capaci di garantire temperature costantemente basse per tutto l'anno.

Señorío de Arínzano

Navarra, Spain

The new structures of this winery estate enclose a historic building ensemble consisting of an old manor, a tower-like warehouse and a small church. Architect Rafael Moneo has created a deliberately heterogeneous structure, whose composition of old and new as well as careful choice of colors and materials nevertheless forms a harmonious whole. Since 1988, Señorío de Arínzano has belonged to the Julián Chivite family, one of the oldest and most important "wine dynasties" of Spain.

Die Neubauten des Weingutes umschließen ein historisches Gebäudeensemble, das aus einem alten Herrenhaus, einem turmartigen Lagergebäude und einer kleinen Kirche besteht. Der Architekt Rafael Moneo schuf damit eine bewusst heterogene Gesamtanlage, die durch ihre sorgfältige Komposition aus Alt und Neu sowie eine sensible Farb- und Materialauswahl dennoch ein harmonisches Ganzes bildet. Señorío de Arínzano gehört seit 1988 zum Besitz der Familie Julián Chivite, einer der ältesten und bedeutendsten „Wein-Dynastien" Spaniens.

Les bâtiments neufs du domaine entourent les trois édifices historiques – une ancienne maison de maître, un chai en forme de tour et une petite église. L'architecte Rafael Moneo a créé ainsi un complexe délibérément hétérogène tout en préservant l'harmonie de l'ensemble, grâce à un équilibre précis entre l'ancien et le moderne et à un choix subtil des couleurs et des matériaux. Señorío de Arínzano appartient depuis 1988 à la famille Julián Chivite, l'une des plus vieilles et des plus grandes « dynasties du vin » en Espagne.

Los edificios nuevos de las bodegas encierran un conjunto arquitectónico histórico, compuesto por una antigua casa señorial, un edifico almacén en forma de torre y una pequeña iglesia. El arquitecto Rafael Moneo creó expresamente un complejo heterogéneo, que a través de su cuidadosa composición entre lo antiguo y lo moderno y de una delicada elección de colores y materiales forma, sin embargo, un todo armonioso. Desde 1988 Señorío de Arínzano es propiedad de la familia Julián Chivite, una de las más antiguas y significativas "dinastías de bodegueros" de España.

I nuovi edifici della tenuta circondano un antico complesso architettonico composto da un'antica casa signorile, un magazzino a forma di torre e una piccola chiesa. L'architetto Rafael Moneo ha così realizzato un complesso volutamente eterogeneo che, giocando sull'accurato accostamento di vecchio e nuovo e sull'attenta scelta di colori e materiali, crea un'unit comunque armoniosa. Dal 1988 Señorío de Arínzano fa parte delle proprietà della famiglia Julián Chivite, una delle più antiche e illustri "dinastie del vino" spagnole.

Don Julián and Don Fernando Chivite López, owners of Señorío de Arínzano

Don Julián und Don Fernando Chivite López, Eigentümer von Señorío de Arínzano

Don Julián et Don Fernando Chivite López, propriétaires de Señorío de Arínzano

Don Julián y Don Fernando Chivite López, propietarios de Señorío de Arínzano

Don Julián e Don Fernando Chivite López, proprietari di Señorío de Arínzano

RESERVA
JULIAN CHIVITE AÑO 1647
Chivite
NAVARRA
DENOMINACION DE ORIGEN
DE PADRES A HIJOS DESDE 1647
COLECCION 125
BODEGAS JULIAN CHIVITE, S.L.
EMBOTELLADO EN LA PROPIEDAD

The new structures of this winery enclose the historic buildings at an angle. A sophisticated wooden construction holds the long-stretching roof framework in place above the wine warehouse.

Die neueren Bauten des Weingutes umschließen winkelförmig die historischen Gebäude. Eine raffinierte Holzkonstruktion trägt den lang gestreckten Dachstuhl über dem Lagerkeller.

Les constructions récentes du domaine encadrent à angle droit les bâtiments historiques. Un ensemble sophistiqué de poutres de bois supporte la charpente toute en longueur au-dessus du chai.

Las nuevas construcciones de las bodegas encierran los edificios históricos formando un ángulo. Una refinada construcción de madera sostiene la armadura alargada del techo de la sala de barricas.

I nuovi edifici della tenuta sono disposti su pianta rettangolare intorno a quelli più antichi. Una raffinata costruzione in legno sostiene l'allungata capriata del tetto che copre la cantina d'invecchiamento.

Weingut Robert Weil

Rheingau, Germany

The namesake of this winery, Dr. Robert Weil, was a professor at the Sorbonne in Paris, before he had to leave France in the run-up to the Franco-German war of 1870/71. In 1875, he purchased a picturesque residence from the Englishman Sir John Sutton in Kiedrich in the German state of Hesse. By purchasing an existing winery as well as some excellent vineyards, he expanded his estate and established the present estate. To this day, the best vineyard of the estate remains the Kiedricher Gräfenberg, whose wines were delivered to the empirical and royal houses of Europe in the late 19th Century.

Der Namensgeber des Weingutes, Dr. Robert Weil, war Professor an der Sorbonne in Paris, bevor er Frankreich im Vorfeld des Deutsch-Französischen Krieges 1870/71 verlassen musste. 1875 erwarb er von dem Engländer Sir John Sutton ein pittoreskes Wohnhaus in Kiedrich. Mit dem Kauf eines bestehenden Weinguts und einiger hervorragender Lagen erweiterte er den Besitz und begründete so das heutige Gut. Die Spitzenlage des Weingutes ist bis heute der Kiedricher Gräfenberg, dessen Weine Ende des 19. Jahrhunderts an die Kaiser- und Königshäuser Europas geliefert wurde.

Le Dr. Robert Weil, qui donna son nom au domaine, était professeur à la Sorbonne à Paris, mais il dut quitter la France à l'aube de la guerre franco-allemande de 1870/71. En 1875, il acheta à l'Anglais Sir John Sutton une pittoresque demeure à Kiedrich. En se portant acquéreur d'un domaine viticole existant et de quelques parcelles exceptionnelles, il étendit sa propriété et fonda ainsi le domaine actuel. Le « Kiedricher Gräfenberg » est considéré aujourd'hui encore comme le meilleur vignoble du domaine et, à la fin du 19ème siècle, ses vins étaient livrés aux cours impériales et royales en Europe.

Quien diera nombre a las bodegas, el Dr. Robert Weil, era profesor en la universidad de la Sorbona, en París, antes de tener que abandonar Francia, ante la inminencia de la guerra francoprusiana de 1870/71. En 1875 adquirió del inglés Sir John Sutton una pintoresca casa en Kiedrich. Con la compra de una bodega ya existente en una magnífica ubicación amplió la finca y fundó lo que es la propiedad actual. La excelente viña de las bodegas sigue siendo hasta hoy la colina Kiedricher Gräfenberg, y en el siglo XIX sus vinos se suministraban a cancilleres y casas reales europeas.

Il Dr. Robert Weil, che diede il nome all'azienda vinicola, era professore alla Sorbona di Parigi, ma dovette lasciare la Francia nel 1870/71, ai primi sentori della Guerra Franco-Tedesca. Nel 1875 acquistò dall'inglese Sir John Sutton una pittoresca villa a Kiedrich, cui successivamente aggiunse una preesistente tenuta ed alcuni eccellenti vigneti, fondando l'attuale azienda vinicola. Ancora oggi il miglior vigneto della tenuta è il Kiedricher Gräfenberg, i cui vini sul finire del XIX secolo rifornivano le case imperiali e reali d'Europa.

Wilhelm Weil,
Director of Weingut Robert Weil

Wilhelm Weil,
Direktor des Weinguts Robert Weil

Wilhelm Weil,
Directeur du Weingut Robert Weil

Wilhelm Weil,
director de Weingut Robert Weil

Wilhelm Weil,
direttore di Weingut Robert Weil

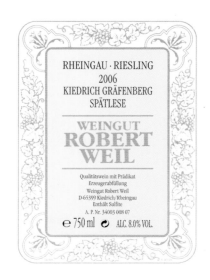

The symbiosis of tradition and modernism, which distinguishes viticulture, is also evident in the interior of the winery.

Die Symbiose von Tradition und Moderne, welche die Weinherstellung prägt, findet sich auch in den Innenräumen des Gutes.

La symbiose des traditions et de la modernité qui caractérise l'élaboration des vins se retrouve dans les intérieurs du manoir.

La simbiosis entre tradición y modernidad que caracteriza a la elaboración del vino se hace también patente en los interiores de la propiedad.

La simbiosi di tradizione e modernità che caratterizza la produzione del vino si ritrova qui anche negli interni della tenuta.

Weingut Dr. Bürklin-Wolf

Palatinate, Germany

This vineyard was founded by Bernhard Bürklin in the 16th Century, making it one of oldest and most traditional wineries in Germany. At least 272 acres of vineyards in the best areas of the Mittelhaardt region also make this winery the largest German winery estate in private ownership. Today, wide parts of this vast complex with its representative manor, historic press-house, vaults and well-groomed gardens and parks can be used for private and cultural events.

Das Weingut wurde im 16. Jahrhundert durch Bernhard Bürklin gegründet – damit zählt es zu den ältesten und traditionsreichsten Weinbaubetrieben in Deutschland. Gut 110 ha Anbauflächen in den besten Lagen der Mittelhaardt machen das Weingut zudem zum größten deutschen Weingut in Privatbesitz. Der großzügige Komplex mit seinem repräsentativen Gutshof, dem historischen Kelterhaus, den Gewölbekellern sowie gepflegten Garten- und Parkanlagen kann heute in weiten Teilen für private und kulturelle Veranstaltungen genutzt werden.

Le domaine fut fondé au 16ème siècle par Bernhard Bürklin – il compte donc parmi les entreprises vinicoles les plus anciennes et les plus porteuses de traditions en Allemagne. Avec au moins 110 hectares de vignobles bénéficiant des meilleures expositions du Mittelhaardt, il est en outre le domaine allemand en propriété privée le plus étendu. Le complexe qui occupe une grande surface et comprend une cour très représentative, un pressoir historique, des caves voûtées ainsi qu'un parc et des jardins soigneusement entretenus, peut accueillir aujourd'hui, dans la plupart de ses bâtiments, des manifestations culturelles et des réceptions privées.

Las bodegas fueron fundadas en el siglo XVI por Bernhard Bürklin, y con ello pertenecen a las empresas vitivinícolas más antiguas y de mayor tradición de Alemania. En torno a 110 hectáreas de plantación ubicadas en las mejores zonas de Mittelhaardt las convierten en una de las mayores bodegas privadas del país. El vasto complejo y su representativa granja, el lagar histórico, las bodegas abovedadas y el cuidado jardín con parque sirven hoy con frecuencia para eventos privados y culturales.

Fondata nel XVI secolo da Bernhard Bürklin, la tenuta è una delle aziende vinicole tedesche più antiche e ricche di tradizione. Circa 110 ettari di superficie coltivata a vite nei migliori siti della regione del Mittelhaardt fanno di lei la più grande tenuta vinicola privata della Germania. Oggi l'imponente complesso, che comprende uno splendido palazzo, lo storico edificio per la torchiatura, le cantine coperte da volte e curatissimi giardini e parchi, può essere in gran parte affittato per eventi privati e manifestazioni culturali.

Bettina Bürklin-von Guradze,
owner of Weingut Dr. Bürklin-Wolf

Bettina Bürklin-von Guradze,
Eigentümerin des Weinguts Dr. Bürklin-Wolf

Bettina Bürklin-von Guradze,
propriétaire du Weingut Dr. Bürklin-Wolf

Bettina Bürklin-von Guradze,
propietaria de Weingut Dr. Bürklin-Wolf

Bettina Bürklin-von Guradze,
proprietaria di Weingut Dr. Bürklin-Wolf

The "Old Stable" of this winery estate underwent renovation in the early 1990s. Ever since, these rooms have been used for large festivities and events. The wide-ranging wooden barrel cellars were built in the 18th Century.

Anfang der 90er-Jahre wurde der „Alte Stall" des Weingutes restauriert. Seither werden diese Räume für größere Feste und Veranstaltungen genutzt. Die weitläufigen Holzfasskeller wurden im 18. Jahrhundert angelegt.

Au début des années 90, la « vieille étable » du domaine a été restaurée. Depuis, ces salles accueillent des réceptions et des manifestations importantes. Les caves à barriques aménagées au 18ème siècle occupent un large espace.

A comienzos de los años 90 se restauró el "Viejo establo" de las bodegas. Desde entonces sus salones se emplean para fiestas y eventos. Las extensas salas de barricas fueron fundadas en el siglo XVIII.

Dopo l'intervento di restauro effettuato agli inizi degli anni Novanta, i locali della "Vecchia Stalla" oggi vengono utilizzati per grandi feste e manifestazioni. Le ampie cantine per la conservazione delle botti in legno risalgono al XVIII secolo.

Rural charm *mingles with unimposing elegance and splendor in the rooms of the winery estate.*

Ländlicher Charme *verbindet sich in den Räumen des Weingutes mit unaufdringlicher Eleganz und Großzügigkeit.*

Dans les pièces du domaine, *un charme campagnard se mêle à une élégance et une aisance discrètes.*

En las estancias de las bodegas *el encanto rural convive con la espaciosidad y una elegancia mesurada.*

Negli storici locali della tenuta *il fascino della campagna convive con eleganza e lusso privi di ostentazione.*

Fürst zu Hohenlohe-Oehringen

Württemberg, Germany

Since 1360, the zu Hohenlohe family has owned the excellent vineyards around the Verrenberg, including the unique vineyard called "Verrenberger Verrenberg". The heavy soil here gives the wine a pronounced sourness and rich extract. Press and fermentation take place at the estate right next to the Verrenberg, whereas maturity and warehousing take place inside the remarkable vaults of the grand residential castle at Öhringen. There, the exquisitely carved bottoms of the barrels point to the long tradition of the winery estate and the family zu Hohenlohe-Oehringen.

Seit 1360 besitzt die Familie zu Hohenlohe die erstklassigen Lagen am Verrenberg, darunter die Monopollage „Verrenberger Verrenberg". Schwere Böden verleihen hier dem Wein eine ausgeprägte Säure und reichlichen Extrakt. Die Kelterung und Gärung finden im Gutshof unmittelbar am Verrenberg statt, Reife und Lagerung hingegen in den eindrucksvollen Kellergewölben des fürstlichen Residenzschlosses zu Öhringen. Dort verweisen prachtvoll geschnitzte Fassböden auf die lange Tradition des Weingutes und der Familie zu Hohenlohe-Oehringen.

La famille zu Hohenlohe possède depuis 1360 les exceptionnelles parcelles du Verrenberg, dont la parcelle en propriété exclusive « Verrenberger Verrenberg ». Des sols lourds confèrent ici au vin une acidité prononcée et un niveau élevé d'extrait. Le pressage du raisin et la fermentation ont lieu au cœur du domaine, au pied du Verrenberg, tandis que la maturation et le stockage se font dans les caves voûtées de la résidence princière d'Öhringen. Là-bas, des fonds de barriques richement sculptés témoignent de la longue tradition du domaine et de la famille zu Hohenlohe-Oehringen.

Desde 1360 la familia zu Hohenlohe es propietaria de las privilegiadas ubicaciones en Verrenberg, entre ellas el monopolio "Verrenberger Verrenberg". Aquí los terrenos duros proporcionan al vino una característica acidez y un rico extracto. El prensado y la fermentación se llevan a cabo en la granja, directamente en Verrenberg, sin embargo la maduración y el almacenamiento tienen lugar en las impresionantes bodegas abovedadas del castillo residencia principesca de Öhringen. Allí las barricas suntuosamente talladas dan muestra de la larga tradición de las bodegas y de la familia Hohenlohe-Oehringen.

Sin dal 1360 la famiglia zu Hohenlohe possiede gli eccellenti vigneti sul Verrenberg, tra cui in esclusiva il "Verrenberger Verrenberg": qui i terreni pesanti conferiscono al vino una decisa acidità ed abbondante estratto. Pigiatura e fermentazione avvengono nella fattoria della tenuta, nelle immediate vicinanze del Verrenberg, all'invecchiamento e stoccaggio invece sono destinate le splendide cantine a volta del castello dei Principi zu Öhringen, dove fondi di botte dalle preziose incisioni ricordano la grande tradizione della tenuta e della famiglia zu Hohenlohe-Oehringen.

Hereditary Prince Kraft zu Hohenlohe-Oehringen, son of Prince Kraft zu Hohenlohe-Oehringen, the owner of the winery

Kraft Erbprinz zu Hohenlohe-Oehringen, der Sohn von Kraft Fürst zu Hohenlohe-Oehringen, dem Eigentümer des Weingutes

Prince héréditaire Kraft zu Hohenlohe-Oehringen, le fils de Prince Kraft zu Hohenlohe-Oehringen, propriétaire du domaine

Príncipe hereditario Kraft zu Hohenlohe-Oehringen, hijo de Príncipe Kraft zu Hohenlohe-Oehringen, propietario de las bodegas

Principe ereditario Kraft zu Hohenlohe-Oehringen, figlio del Kraft Principe zu Hohenlohe-Oehringen, proprietario della tenuta

Fürst zu Hohenlohe-Oehringen

Verrenberger Verrenberg

RIESLING SPÄTLESE TROCKEN

2006

The exquisitely carved bottoms of the barrels in the cellar of the grand residential castle point to the great history of the winery estate and of the family zu Hohenlohe-Oehringen.

Die prachtvoll geschnitzten Fassböden im Keller des fürstlichen Residenzschlosses verweisen auf die große Geschichte des Weingutes und der Familie zu Hohenlohe-Oehringen.

Dans la cave de la résidence princière, les fonds de barriques richement sculptés témoignent de la grande tradition du domaine et de la famille zu Hohenlohe-Oehringen.

En la bodega del castillo principesco las barricas suntuosamente talladas documentan la gran historia del dominio y de la familia Hohenlohe-Oehringen.

I fondi di botte dalle preziose incisioni, conservati nelle cantine del principesco castello, rimandano alla grande storia della tenuta e della famiglia zu Hohenlohe-Oehringen.

Weingut Leo Hillinger

Burgenland, Austria

Completed in 2004, most of the state-of-the-art premises of the Leo Hillinger winery has been laid out underground. Only the spectacular tasting room stands out, held by narrow V-shaped pillars, in the middle of the vineyards of Jois near the Neusiedler Lake. Leo Hillinger, who took over the winery from his father in 1990 at the age of 23, diligently turned his ideas of state-of-the-art vinification into reality with the rebuilding of the estate.

Das 2004 fertiggestellte, hochmoderne Betriebsgebäude des Weingutes Leo Hillinger wurde zum größten Teil unterirdisch angelegt. Lediglich der spektakuläre Verkostungsraum erhebt sich, von schlanken V-förmigen Stützen getragen, inmitten der Weinberge von Jois am Neusiedler See. Leo Hillinger, der das Weingut 1990 im Alter von 23 Jahren von seinem Vater übernommen hat, verwirklichte mit dem Neubau des Gutshofs konsequent seine Vorstellungen von modernster Vinifikation.

L'essentiel du bâtiment d'exploitation ultramoderne du domaine Leo Hillinger, dont la construction s'est achevée en 2004, a été enterré. Seul l'espace de dégustation spectaculaire est comme suspendu, porté par de fins piliers en V, au milieu des vignes de Jois près du lac Neusiedler. Leo Hillinger, qui a repris le domaine en 1990 à la suite de son père, à l'âge de 23 ans, a concrétisé, sans compromis, sa conception d'une vinification des plus modernes par la construction de ce bâtiment.

El moderno edificio industrial de las bodegas Leo Hillinger, concluido en 2004, es en su mayor parte subterráneo. Únicamente la espectacular sala de catas se levanta sostenida por estrechos apoyos en forma de V, en medio de los viñedos de Jois, ubicados en el lago Neusiedler. Con la nueva construcción del edificio, Leo Hillinger, que en 1990 con tan sólo 23 años se hizo cargo de las bodegas de su padre, ha hecho realidad de forma consecuente su clara idea de vinificación moderna.

La cantina di vinificazione della tenuta Leo Hillinger, finita di costruire nel 2004, è per la maggior parte sotterranea: in mezzo ai vigneti di Jois, sul Lago di Neusiedl, si erge solo la spettacolare sala di degustazione, poggiata su snelli pilastri a V. Leo Hillinger, subentrato al padre nella guida dell'azienda all'età di 23 anni, con la costruzione della nuova cantina è riuscito a concretizzare con coerenza la sua idea di moderna vinificazione.

Leo Hillinger, owner of the winery of the same name

Leo Hillinger, der Eigentümer des gleichnamigen Weingutes

Leo Hillinger, propriétaire du domaine du même nom

Leo Hillinger, propietario de las bodegas del mismo nombre

Leo Hillinger, proprietario dell' omonima azienda vinicola

The thoroughly modern design of the building and interior makes the design of the gerner°gerner plus architect's office an all-around complex work of art.

Die konsequent moderne Gestaltung von Gebäude und Innenräumen macht den Bau der Architekten gerner°gerner plus zu einem komplexen Gesamtkunstwerk.

La conception moderne, sans concession, des bâtiments et des intérieurs fait de cet édifice, créé par les architectes gerner°gerner plus, une œuvre d'art totale complexe.

La unitaria decoración moderna de los edificios y sus interiores convierte la construcción de los arquitectos gerner°gerner plus en una completa obra de arte.

L'allestimento coerentemente moderno dell'edificio e degli interni fa del progetto degli architetti gerner°gerner plus una complessa opera d'arte totale.

Weingut Leo Hillinger *Burgenland, Austria* 131

Alois Lageder

South Tyrol, Italy

The Alois Lageder winery—founded in 1855 by Lageder's great grandfather in Bolzano and continuously expanded by the successive generations—includes the winery estates of Tór Löwengang (since 1934) and Casòn Hirschprunn (since 1991) as well as the Vinotheque Im Paradeis. Alois Lageder combines state-of-the-art technological and ecological methods for growing wine with a comprehensive quality philosophy that cultivates not only the production of excellent brand wines and Cuvées, but also an intensive connection to the fine arts and music.

Zur Kellerei Alois Lageder – 1855 von dessen Urgroßvater in Bozen gegründet und in den Folgegenerationen kontinuierlich erweitert – gehören die Weingüter Tór Löwengang (seit 1934) und Casòn Hirschprunn (seit 1991) sowie die Vinotheque Im Paradeis. Alois Lageder vereint modernste technologische und ökologische Methoden im Weinbau mit einer umfassenden Qualitäts-Philosophie, die über die Produktion von hervorragenden Sortenweinen und Cuvées hinaus eine intensive Verbindung mit der bildenden Kunst und der Musik pflegt.

La cave Alois Lageder – fondée en 1855 par son arrière-grand-père à Bozen et continuellement agrandie par les générations suivantes – comprend les domaines de Tór Löwengang (depuis 1934) et de Casòn Hirschprunn (depuis 1991) ainsi que la vinothèque Im Paradeis. Alois Lageder met en œuvre des moyens technologiques et écologiques de pointe dans la culture de la vigne et les conjugue avec une profonde philosophie de la qualité. Cette philosophie va bien au-delà de la production de vins monovariétaux et de cuvées exceptionnelles, et entretient des liens très forts avec les beaux-arts et la musique.

A las bodegas de Alois Lageder, fundadas por su bisabuelo en Bozen en 1855 y ampliadas continuamente por las generaciones posteriores, pertenecen Tór Löwengang (desde 1934) y Casòn Hirschprunn (desde 1991) así como la Vinotheque Im Paradeis. Alois Lageder concilia los más modernos métodos tecnológicos y ecológicos existentes en la producción vitivinícola con una completa filosofía de calidad, que además de la creación de excelentes vino de selección y Cuvées mantiene una relación intensiva con las bellas artes y la música.

Le Cantine Alois Lageder – fondate nel 1855 dal bisnonno a Bolzano e continuamente ampliate nelle generazioni successive – comprendono le tenute Tór Löwengang (dal 1934) e Casòn Hirschprunn (dal 1991), nonché la Vinotheque Im Paradeis. Alois Lageder riunisce i più moderni metodi tecnologici ed ecologici di vinicoltura con un filosofia complessiva della qualità, che oltre alla produzione di eccellenti vini monovitigno e cuvée cura un intenso legame con le arti figurative e la musica.

Alois Lageder, owner of the winery of the same name

Alois Lageder, der Eigentümer des gleichnamigen Weingutes

Alois Lageder, propriétaire du domaine du même nom

Alois Lageder, propietario de las bodegas del mismo nombre

Alois Lageder, proprietario dell' omonima tenuta

Modern art in the new Tòr Löwengang premises are as much part of the Alois Lageder winery as the historic quarters and romantic niches of the Casòn Hirschprunn.

Moderne Kunst im neuen Betriebsgebäude von Tòr Löwengang gehört ebenso zum Weingut Alois Lageder wie die historischen Räume und romantischen Winkel des Casòn Hirschprunn.

L'art moderne dans le nouveau bâtiment d'exploitation du domaine de Tòr Löwengang fait partie intégrante de la cave Alois Lageder, au même titre que les salles historiques et le coin romantique du domaine de Casòn Hirschprunn.

En las bodegas Alois Lageder el arte moderno de los nuevos edificios de Tòr Löwengang convive con las estancias históricas y el romántico rincón del Casòn Hirschprunn.

L'arte moderna che domina nel nuovo edificio di Tòr Löwengang è parte integrante della tenuta esattamente quanto gli storici locali e gli angoli romantici del Casòn Hirschprunn.

MANINCOR

South Tyrol, Italy

In 1608, Hieronymus Manincor zu Ehrenhausen built this awe-inspiring historic estate above Kalterer Lake. In 1977, the estate came under the ownership of Count Michael Goëss-Enzenberg, who transformed the largest supplier of grapes in southern Tyrol into an independent winery estate. Its new aspiration and image are vividly reflected in the winery's modern cellar structures, which were commissioned in early 2004. These combine a modern interpretation of architecture with a profound sense of tradition, nature and landscape.

Das eindrucksvolle historische Gutshaus wurde 1608 von Hieronymus Manincor zu Ehrenhausen oberhalb des Kalterer Sees errichtet. 1977 ging das Gut in den Besitz von Michael Graf Goëss-Enzenberg über, der aus dem zuvor größten Traubenlieferanten Südtirols ein eigenständiges Weingut formte. Sichtbarer Ausdruck des neuen Anspruchs und Selbstverständnisses sind die modernen Kelleranlagen des Weingutes, die im Frühjahr 2004 in Betrieb genommen wurden. In ihnen verbindet sich eine moderne Architekturauffassung mit einem ausgeprägten Sinn für Tradition, Natur und Landschaft.

Le manoir historique imposant fut construit en 1608 par Hieronymus Manincor zu Ehrenhausen, en amont du lac de Caldaro. La propriété revint en 1977 au comte Michael Goëss-Enzenberg qui transforma en domaine viticole indépendant ce qui était auparavant le plus grand fournisseur de raisins du Tyrol du Sud. Son ambition évidente de produire des vins prestigieux se traduisit dans la construction d'une cave moderne, inaugurée au printemps 2004. Celle-ci reflète également une conception moderne de l'architecture respectant profondément la tradition, la nature et le paysage.

La impresionante casa señorial histórica fue fundada en 1608 por Hieronymus Manincor zu Ehrenhausen sobre el lago di Caldaro. En 1977, la propiedad pasó a conde Michael Goëss-Enzenberg, que convirtió al que había sido el mayor suministrador de uva en Tirol del Sur en una verdadera bodega. Una muestra visible de las nuevas exigencias y necesidades de la propiedad son los modernos espacios de bodegas, puestos en funcionamiento a comienzos de 2004. En ellos se concilian el principio de arquitectura moderna con un marcado sentido de la tradición, la naturaleza y el paisaje.

La splendida dimora storica fu fatta costruire nel 1608 sopra al Lago di Caldara da Hieronymus Manincor zu Ehrenhausen. Nel 1977 la tenuta divenne proprietà del conte Michael Goëss-Enzenberg, il quale trasformò quello che allora era il più grande fornitore d'uva dell'Alto Adige in un'azienda vitivinicola indipendente. Danno prova anche visiva della rinnovata ambizione ed immagine di sé della tenuta le nuove cantine, entrate in funzione nel 2004: qui una moderna concezione architettonica si fonde con uno spiccato senso della tradizione, della natura e del territorio.

*Count **Michael Goëss-Enzenberg** and his wife Sophie, owners of MANINCOR*

***Michael Graf Goëss-Enzenberg** und seine Frau Sophie, Eigentümer von MANINCOR*

*Comte **Michael Goëss-Enzenberg** et sa femme Sophie, propriétaires de MANINCOR*

*Conde **Michael Goëss-Enzenberg** y su esposa Sophie, propietarios de MANINCOR*

*Conte **Michael Goëss-Enzenberg** e sua moglie Sophie, proprietari di MANINCOR*

The new cellar by architects Walter Angonese, Rainer Köberl and Silvia Boday is mostly situated underground.

Das neue Kellergebäude der Architekten Walter Angonese, Rainer Köberl und Silvia Boday liegt weitgehend unter der Erde.

La nouvelle cave conçue par les architectes Walter Angonese, Rainer Köberl et Silvia Boday est en grande partie enterrée.

Los nuevos edificios de las bodegas de los arquitectos Walter Angonese, Rainer Köberl y Silvia Boday son construcciones subterráneas.

Il nuovo edificio per le cantine realizzato dagli architetti Walter Angonese, Rainer Köberl e Silvia Boday si trova in gran parte sotto terra.

This ensures optimal climate conditions and does not impose on the landscape around the Kalterer Lake.

Dies garantiert optimale klimatische Bedingungen und bewahrt den Landschaftsraum am Kalterer See.

Ceci garantit des conditions climatiques optimales et préserve les paysages environnants du lac de Caldaro.

Con ello se garantizan condiciones climáticas óptimas y se mantiene la armonía del paisaje en torno al lago Kalterer.

Questo garantisce ideali condizioni climatiche senza venire a intaccare la bellezza paesaggistica del lago di Caldaro.

Fontanafredda

Piedmont, Italy

The awe-inspiring Fontanafredda estate can be traced back to King Victor Emmanuel II., who acquired vast areas of land here in the mid-19th Century. His son, Emmanuel Guerrieri, founded the winery estate bearing the same name in 1878. The vast complex with its lavishly furnished interior is rich in historicism and Art Noveau. Owned by the Monte dei Paschi di Siena Bank since 1931, in recent years, the way ahead has been cleared for wine cultivation at Fontanafredda by modernizing cultivation methods, cellars as well as hiring a new vintner.

Der eindrucksvolle Gutsbesitz Fontanafredda geht zurück auf König Viktor Emanuel II., der hier Mitte des 19. Jahrhunderts weitläufige Ländereien erwarb. Sein Sohn Emanuel Guerrieri gründete 1878 das gleichnamige Weingut. Die großzügige Anlage mit ihren reich ausgestatteten Innenräumen atmet den Geist von Historismus und Jugendstil. Seit 1931 im Besitz der Bank Monte dei Paschi di Siena, erlebte der Weinbau auf Fontanafredda in den vergangenen Jahren mit modernisierten Anbaumethoden, Kellereianlagen und einem neuen Kellermeister einen Aufbruch in die Zukunft.

L'impressionnant domaine foncier de Fontanafredda remonte au roi Victor-Emmanuel II, qui y acheta de grandes surfaces de terres au milieu du 19ème siècle. Son fils Emmanuel Guerrieri fonda en 1878 le domaine du même nom. La grande bâtisse, avec ses intérieurs richement aménagés, est habitée par le souffle de l'historisme et de l'Art Nouveau. La banque Monte dei Paschi di Siena en est propriétaire depuis 1931 et la culture de la vigne à Fontanafredda a connu ces dernières années un nouvel essor grâce à la modernisation des méthodes de culture et des caves, et à l'arrivée d'un nouveau caviste.

El imponente dominio de Fontanafredda proviene de la época del rey Víctor Manuel II., que a mediados del siglo XIX adquirió aquí grandes terrenos. En 1878 su hijo Manuel Guerrieri fundó las bodegas del mismo nombre. La extensa construcción de interiores completamente equipados respira un espíritu de historicismo y Modernismo. Después de pasar a ser propiedad del banco Monte dei Paschi di Siena en 1931, las bodegas de Fontanafredda han vivido en los últimos años un salto al futuro a través de métodos de producción modernizados y naves para bodegas y bodeguero nuevos.

Le origini dell'imponente tenuta di Fontanafredda risalgono alla metà del XIX secolo, quando il re Vittorio Emanuele II acquistò qui estesi possedimenti terrieri; fu poi suo figlio, Emanuele Guerrieri, a fondare l'omonima azienda vinicola nel 1878. Nel lussuoso palazzo, dagli interni riccamente decorati, aleggia ancora lo spirito della storia e dello stile liberty. Dal 1931 proprietà del Monte dei Paschi di Siena, negli scorsi anni Fontanafredda ha visto la viticoltura proiettarsi nel futuro, grazie all'impiego di innovativi metodi di coltivazione, all'allestimento di moderne cantine di vinificazione e all'assunzione di un nuovo enologo.

The management of Fontanafredda (left to right): Giovanni Minetti, Alberto Grasso, Marinella Maiorano, Paris Renzini, Roberto Bruno

Die Geschäftsführung von Fontanafredda (von links nach rechts): Giovanni Minetti, Alberto Grasso, Marinella Maiorano, Paris Renzini, Roberto Bruno

Les dirigeants de Fontanafredda (de gauche à droite) : Giovanni Minetti, Alberto Grasso, Marinella Maiorano, Paris Renzini, Roberto Bruno

El equipo de dirección de Fontanafredda (de izquierda a derecha): Giovanni Minetti, Alberto Grasso, Marinella Maiorano, Paris Renzini y Roberto Bruno

La direzione amministrativa di Fontanafredda (da sinistra a destra): Giovanni Minetti, Alberto Grasso, Marinella Maiorano, Paris Renzini, Roberto Bruno

The "royal" past of this winery estate is still reflected today in the noble structures, vast cellars and stylish interior of Fontanafredda.

Die „königliche" Vergangenheit des Weingutes spiegelt sich bis heute in den noblen Bauten, den ausgedehnten Kelleranlagen und den stilvollen Interieurs von Fontanafredda.

Le passé « royal » du domaine se reflète aujourd'hui encore dans les bâtiments aristocratiques, les caves très étendues et les intérieurs de bon goût de Fontanafredda.

El pasado "real" del dominio se refleja aún hoy en las nobles construcciones de las vastas bodegas y el estilo de los interiores de Fontanafredda.

I trascorsi "reali" della tenuta si rispecchiano fino ad oggi nei nobili edifici, nelle ampie cantine e negli interni eleganti di Fontanafredda.

Marchesi di Barolo

Piedmont, Italy

Founded in 1861, this winery originally belonged to the Marchesi Falletti family, which, in the early 19th Century, created the wine that enjoys world fame today as "Barolo". Since 1970, the Castello has been under local ownership, which has established a wine museum at the site. The winery estate, which is located at the center of Barolo, presently belongs to the Abbona family, which purchased it in the late 19th Century. In addition to the shops and tasting rooms, it also houses a wine library and an exclusive restaurant.

Das 1861 gegründete Weingut war ursprünglich im Besitz der Familie der Marchesi Falletti, die zu Beginn des 19. Jahrhunderts den Wein schuf, der heute unter dem Namen „Barolo" Weltruhm genießt. Seit 1970 befindet sich das Castello im Besitz der Gemeinde, die dort ein Weinmuseum eingerichtet hat. Das Weingut, das sich im Zentrum Barolos befindet, gehört heute der Familie Abbona, die es Ende des 19. Jahrhunderts erwarb. Neben den Verkaufs- und Probierräumen befinden sich dort eine Weinbibliothek sowie ein exklusives Restaurant.

Le domaine fondé en 1861 appartenait à l'origine à la famille des Marchesi Falletti qui créa, au début du 19ème siècle, le vin de réputation mondiale appelé « Barolo ». Depuis 1970, le Castello est la propriété de la commune qui y a installé un musée du vin. Le domaine qui se trouve au centre de Barolo appartient aujourd'hui à la famille Abbona, qui l'a acheté à la fin du 19ème siècle. On y trouve, outre la salle de dégustation et l'espace de vente, une bibliothèque du vin ainsi qu'un restaurant exclusif.

Las bodegas fundadas en 1861 pertenecían en origen a la familia de los Marquéses Falletti, que a comienzos del siglo XIX crearon el vino que hoy disfruta de fama mundial bajo la denominación de "Barolo". Desde 1970 el Castello es propiedad del municipio, que lo ha convertido en museo del vino. Las bodegas, ubicadas en el centro del Barolo, pertenecen actualmente a la familia Abbona, que las adquirió a finales del XIX. Junto a las salas de cata y venta existe además una biblioteca del vino y un exclusivo restaurante.

La tenuta, fondata nel 1861, fu originariamente proprietà della famiglia dei Marchesi Falletti, che verso l'inizio dell'Ottocento avevano creato quel vino che oggi col nome di "Barolo" gode di fama mondiale. Dal 1970 il castello è stato acquisito dal Comune, che vi ha allestito un'enoteca storica. La tenuta vinicola, che si trova al centro della cittadina di Barolo, oggi appartiene alla famiglia Abbona, che l'acquistò gia sul finire del XIX secolo: qui, oltre ai locali destinati alla vendita e alla degustazione, si trovano anche una biblioteca enologica e un esclusivo ristorante.

Ernesto and Anna Abbona,
the owners of Marchesi di Barolo

Ernesto und Anna Abbona,
die Eigentümer von Marchesi di Barolo

Ernesto et Anna Abbona,
propriétaires de Marchesi di Barolo

Ernesto y Anna Abbona,
propietarios de Marchesi di Barolo

Ernesto e Anna Abbona,
proprietari di Marchesi di Barolo

The wine boutique houses one of the most voluminous collections of Barolo wines in the world. Every year, the 35,000 bottles of the collection are supplemented by about 400 bottles of the new vintage.

In der Vinothek lagert eine der weltweit umfangreichsten Sammlungen von Barolo-Weinen. Die 35.000 Flaschen der Kollektion werden jährlich um ca. 400 Flaschen des neuen Jahrgangs ergänzt.

Dans la vinothèque repose une des collections les plus vastes au monde de vins Barolo. Les 35 000 bouteilles de la collection se voient ajouter chaque année quelque 400 bouteilles du dernier millésime.

En la vinoteca reposa una de las mayores colecciones mundiales de vinos de Barolo. Las 35.000 botellas de la colección se completan cada año con 400 botellas de la nueva cosecha.

Nella vinoteca è immagazzinata una delle più complete collezioni di Barolo del mondo. Ogni anno alle 35.000 bottiglie della collezione se ne aggiungono circa 400 della nuova vendemmia.

Castello di Verduno

Piedmont, Italy

In 1909, the Burlotto family purchased the former hunting seat of Castello di Verduno from ownership of the House of Savoy. Ever since the 1950s, the family has used the early 16th Century structure to operate a hotel and to produce excellent Barolo and Verduno wines in its historic vaults. The picturesque estate is a particularly exquisite combination of rural Piedmont charm and of the historic atmosphere of the Castello.

Im Jahre 1909 erwarb die Familie Burlotto das ehemalige Jagdschloss Castello di Verduno aus dem Besitz des Hauses Savoyen. Seit den 50er-Jahren betreibt die Familie in dem Bau aus dem frühen 16. Jahrhundert ein Hotel und produziert in den historischen Kellergewölben hervorragende Barolo- und Verduno-Weine. In der malerischen Anlage verbinden sich der ländliche Charme des Piemonts und das historische Ambiente des Castellos zu einer Mischung von ganz besonderem Reiz.

En 1909, la famille Burlotto acheta l'ancien pavillon de chasse Castello di Verduno, un des biens de la maison de Savoie. Depuis les années 50, la famille gère un hôtel dans le bâtiment du début du 16ème siècle et produit dans les caves voûtées historiques les fameux vins Barolo et Verduno. Ce domaine pittoresque est imprégné du charme campagnard piémontais et de l'ambiance historique du château, ce qui le rend particulièrement attrayant.

En el año 1909 la familia Burlotto adquirió la antigua mansión de caza Castello di Verduno, perteneciente a la casa de Saboya. Desde los años 50, en la construcción de principios del siglo XVI la familia rige un hotel y en sus bodegas abovedadas produce excelentes vinos Barolo y Verduno. En el pintoresco recinto se entremezclan el encanto de la campaña piamontesa y el ambiente histórico del Castello creando un atractivo muy especial.

La famiglia Burlotto acquistò nel 1909 il Castello di Verduno, a suo tempo castello di caccia dei Savoia, e dagli anni Cinquanta ha trasformato l'edificio, risalente agli inizi del XVI secolo, in un albergo da lei stessa diretto. Contemporaneamente nelle antiche cantine coperte a volta della tenuta si producono eccellenti vini delle qualità Barolo e Verduno. Nel pittoresco complesso il fascino della campagna piemontese e lo storico ambiente del castello si fondono creando un'atmosfera unica.

Three generations of the Burlotto family

Drei Generationen der Burlotto-Familie

Trois générations de la famille Burlotto

Tres generaciones de la familia Burlotto

Tre generazioni della famiglia Burlotto

The Castello di Verduno *is distinguished by its unpretentious, casual elegance. The historic complex is also used as a restaurant and hotel.*

Das Castello di Verduno *zeichnet sich durch unprätentiöse, legere Eleganz aus. Die historische Anlage wird auch als Restaurant und Hotel genutzt.*

Le Castello di Verduno *se distingue par son élégance naturelle et sans prétention. La propriété historique accueille également un restaurant et un hôtel.*

El Castello di Verduno *se caracteriza por su elegancia ligera y sin pretensiones. El edificio histórico alberga un restaurante y un hotel.*

Caratteristica del Castello di Verduno *è l'eleganza senza pretese, quasi impalpabile; lo storico complesso funge anche da ristorante e albergo.*

Badia a Coltibuono

Chianti, Italy

This winery is based on the Benedictine monastery "Cultus Boni", which was erected by monks of the Vallombrosa Abbey in the year 1051. It was also those monks who began to cultivate wine, whose excellent reputation has been recorded as far back as the Renaissance. In 1810, Napoleon Bonaparte expropriated the monastery. In 1846, the estate came under the ownership of banker Michele Giutini, an ancestor of the current owner, Emanuela Stucchi Prinetti. Since the early 1990s, the estate has also come to be known as a cooking school for Tuscan specialties.

Das Weingut geht auf das Benediktinerkloster „Cultus Boni" zurück, das 1051 durch Mönche der Abtei Vallombrosa erbaut wurde. Diese begannen auch mit dem Anbau von Wein, dessen hervorragender Ruf schon in der Renaissance belegt ist. 1810 wurde das Kloster durch Napoleon Bonaparte enteignet. 1846 ging das Gut schließlich in den Besitz des Bankiers Michele Giutini über, einem Vorfahren der heutigen Eigentümerin Emanuela Stucchi Prinetti. Seit Anfang der 90er-Jahre ist das Gut auch als Kochschule für toskanische Spezialitäten bekannt.

L'origine du domaine viticole remonte au monastère bénédictin du « Cultus Boni » qui fut fondé en 1051 par les moines de l'abbaye de Vallombrosa. Ceux-ci lancèrent aussi la culture de la vigne dont la réputation exceptionnelle est documentée dès la Renaissance. En 1810, Napoléon Bonaparte expropria le monastère. En 1846, le domaine revint finalement au banquier Michele Giutini, aïeul de l'actuelle propriétaire, Emanuela Stucchi Prinetti. Depuis le début des années 90, le domaine est également connu pour son école de cuisine dédiée aux spécialités toscanes.

La propiedad vitícola se remonta al monasterio benedictino de "Cultus Boni", construido en 1051 por los monjes de la abadía de Vallombrosa. Fueron ellos quienes comenzaron también con la producción de vino, cuya excelente fama aparece ya documentada durante el Renacimiento. En 1810 Napoleón Bonaparte expropia el monasterio y en 1846 la propiedad pasa a manos del banquero Michele Giutini, un antepasado de la actual propietaria, Emanuela Stucchi Prinetti. Desde comienzos de los años 90 el dominio tiene además fama como escuela de cocina toscana.

La tenuta ha le sue origini nel monastero benedettino di "Cultus Boni", costruito nel 1051 da monaci dell'Abbazia di Vallombrosa, gli stessi che qui diedero anche inizio alla viticoltura, producendo un vino la cui eccellente fama è documentata fin dal Rinascimento. Il monastero, espropriato da Napoleone Bonaparte nel 1810, nel 1846 divenne proprietà del banchiere Michele Giutini, antenato dell'attuale proprietaria, Emanuela Stucchi Prinetti. Dagli inizi degli anni Novanta la tenuta è nota anche come scuola di cucina per specialità gastronomiche toscane.

Emanuela Stucchi Prinetti,
owner of Badia a Coltibuono

Emanuela Stucchi Prinetti,
Eigentümerin von Badia a Coltibuono

Emanuela Stucchi Prinetti,
propriétaire de Badia a Coltibuono

Emanuela Stucchi Prinetti,
propietaria de Badia a Coltibuono

Emanuela Stucchi Prinetti,
proprietaria di Badia a Coltibuono

The gardens of the Badia a Coltibuono have been restored to their original form as a monastic kitchen garden. Geometrically groomed hedges subdivide beds with spices and medicinal herbs.

Die Gartenanlagen der Badia a Coltibuono sind heute in ihrer ursprünglichen Form als klösterlicher Nutzgarten wiederhergestellt. Geometrisch geschnittene Hecken unterteilen Beete mit Gewürzen und medizinischen Kräutern.

Les jardins de Badia a Coltibuono ont retrouvé aujourd'hui leur forme et leur fonction initiales, c'est-à-dire verger et potager du monastère. Des haies taillées géométriquement délimitent les plates-bandes où poussent aromates et herbes médicinales.

En la actualidad, los jardines de Badia a Coltibuono se han recreado en su forma original como jardines funcionales de monasterio. Los setos recortados geométricamente dividen bancales con especias y hierbas medicinales.

I giardini della Badia a Coltibuono sono oggi tornati alla loro vocazione erboristica, come originariamente voluto dai monaci: siepi potate in forma geometrica suddividono aiuole in cui crescono spezie e piante medicinali.

The living quarters, adorned with frescos, keep the spirit of the old monastery structures alive to this day.

In den mit Fresken geschmückten Wohnräumen ist bis heute der Geist der ehemaligen Klosteranlagen spürbar.

Dans les pièces d'habitation décorées de fresques flotte encore aujourd'hui l'esprit de l'ancien aménagement monacal.

Los habitáculos adornados con frescos retienen hasta el día de hoy el espíritu del antiguo monasterio.

Nelle sale interne, adorne di affreschi, si respira ancora oggi lo spirito dell'antica abbazia.

Barone Ricasoli

Chianti, Italy

For more than 900 years, the Castello di Brolio has been the original estate of the Ricasoli family, whose most famous representative—Baron Bettino Ricasoli—was the first to formulate the perfect composition and pressing of the "Chianti Classico" in the second half of the 19th Century. The significant history of the castle, erected in 1860 on fortification walls from the 16th Century, is reflected in its remarkable, richly furnished interior. The actual winery estate is located at the foot of the hill and its gigantic cellars hold the produce of about 618 acres of vineyards so it can mature into fine wines.

Castello di Brolio ist seit über 900 Jahren Stammsitz der Familie Ricasoli, deren berühmtester Vertreter – Baron Bettino Ricasoli – in der zweiten Hälfte des 19. Jahrhunderts als erster die optimale Zusammensetzung und Kelterung des „Chianti Classico" formulierte. Die bedeutende Geschichte des Schlosses, das 1860 auf Festungsmauern aus dem 16. Jahrhundert erbaut wurde, spiegelt sich in den eindrucksvollen, reich ausgestatten Innenräumen wieder. Am Fuße des Hügels liegt das eigentliche Weingut, in dessen riesigen Kelleranlagen der Ertrag von rund 250 ha Rebfläche zu edlen Weinen reift.

Depuis plus de 900 ans, le Castello di Brolio est le siège de la famille Ricasoli, dont le représentant le plus célèbre – le baron Bettino Ricasoli – formula, dans la deuxième moitié du 19ème siècle, la composition et la vinification idéales du « Chianti Classico ». La remarquable histoire du château, édifié en 1860 sur des murs de fortification datant du 16ème siècle, se reflète dans les intérieurs imposants, richement aménagés. Le domaine proprement dit s'étend au pied de la colline et, dans ses caves immenses, la récolte d'environ 250 hectares de vignes deviendra des vins fins au terme d'une longue maturation.

Castello di Brolio es propiedad de la familia Ricasoli desde hace más de 900 años. Su representante más conocido, el barón Bettino Ricasoli, dio con la fórmula de composición óptima para el prensado del "Chianti Classico". La significativa historia del castillo, construido en 1860 sobre las murallas de una fortaleza del siglo XVI, se refleja en los impresionantes salones ricamente decorados. La auténtica bodega se levanta al pie de la colina; en sus enormes espacios de bodegas madura el fruto de 250 hectáreas de viñedo, de donde resulta el refinado vino.

Il Castello di Brolio è da oltre novecento anni la sede ufficiale della famiglia Ricasoli, il cui rappresentante più famoso, il barone Bettino Ricasoli, nella seconda metà del XIX secolo fu il primo a definire la composizione e vinificazione ideale del "Chianti Classico". La notevole storia del castello, costruito nel 1860 sulle fondamenta di una fortezza del XVI secolo, si rispecchia negli interni, imponenti nel loro ricco arredamento. Ai piedi della collina si trova l'azienda vinicola vera e propria, nelle cui gigantesche cantine il prodotto di circa 250 ettari di vigneti matura per tramutarsi infine in vino eccellente.

Francesco Ricasoli, the 32nd Baron of Brolio

Francesco Ricasoli, der 32ste Baron von Brolio

Francesco Ricasoli, le 32ème baron de Brolio

Francesco Ricasoli, el trigesimosegundo barón de Brolio

Francesco Ricasoli, il 32esimo barone di Brolio

The primary wine of Ricasoli is the "Chianti Classico Castello di Brolio" made of 100% Sangiovese, which is matured for more than 18 months in Barrique barrels.

Hauptwein von Ricasoli ist der „Chianti Classico Castello di Brolio" aus 100% Sangiovese-Trauben, der über 18 Monate in Barrique-Fässern ausgebaut wird.

Le principal vin de Ricasoli est le « Chianti Classico Castello di Brolio » issu à 100% de grappes de sangiovese et qui passe plus de 18 mois en barriques.

El principal vino de Ricasoli es el "Chianti Classico Castello di Brolio", 100% de uva Sangiovese, con 18 meses de crianza en barricas de roble.

Il vino principale di Ricasoli è il "Chianti Classico Castello di Brolio" che, ricavato al 100% da vitigni Sangiovese, matura in barrique per più di 18 mesi.

The Ricasoli barons' political power of yore is evident to this day in the splendid interior of the Castello di Brolio.

Von der einstigen politischen Macht der Barone Ricasoli zeugen bis heute die prächtigen Innenräume des Castello di Brolio.

Les somptueux intérieurs du Castello di Brolio témoignent aujourd'hui encore de l'ancienne puissance politique des barons Ricasoli.

Las opulentas salas del Castello de Brolio testifican el poder político que tuvo en su día el barón de Ricasoli.

I sontuosi interni del Castello di Brolio sono ancora oggi la prova evidente del passato potere politico dei baroni Ricasoli.

Castello di Fonterutoli
Chianti, Italy

Under the ownership of the Mazzei family since 1435, this winery has retained its peaceful, village-like character to this day: It consists of a handful of houses, the San Miniato Church and the villa with its well-groomed gardens, which replaced the original castle in the late 16th Century. The interior of the villa has an air of both rustic and refined elegance. The winery has just recently been equipped with new cellars, which are on the cutting edge of technology, both in ecological and enological terms.

Seit 1435 im Besitz der Familie Mazzei, hat sich das Gut bis heute einen friedlichen, dörflichen Charakter bewahrt: Es umfasst eine Handvoll Häuser, die Kirche San Miniato und die Villa mit ihren gepflegten Gartenanlagen, die Ende des 16. Jahrhunderts an Stelle des ursprünglichen Kastells errichtet wurde. Die Innenräume der Villa zeugen von rustikaler, gleichwohl gediegener Eleganz. Gerade erst fertiggestellt wurden die neuen Kellereianlagen des Weingutes, die sowohl ökologisch wie önologisch auf modernstem Stand sind.

Depuis 1435 aux mains de la famille Mazzei, le domaine a su préserver jusqu'à ce jour son caractère de village paisible. Il comprend une poignée de maisons, l'église San Miniato et la villa entourée de jardins bien entretenus, qui fut construite à la fin du 16ème siècle à la place du château d'origine. Les intérieurs de la villa affichent une rusticité non dénuée d'élégance. La nouvelle cave du domaine, dont la construction vient de s'achever, met en œuvre le meilleur des technologies tant en matière écologique qu'œnologique.

El dominio, que desde 1435 ha pertenecido a la familia Mazzei, conserva hasta hoy su carácter rural y sosegado. El lugar comprende un puñado de casas, la iglesia de Miniato y la mansión con sus vistosos jardines, concebida a finales del siglo XVI para sustituir al castillo original. Los interiores de la mansión son imagen de elegancia rústica y pura a la vez. Las nuevas instalaciones de las bodegas, recientemente concluidas, funcionan al más alto nivel tecnológico desde el punto de vista enológico y ecológico.

Dal 1435 proprietà della famiglia Mazzei, questa tenuta ha mantenuto fino ad oggi il suo carattere tranquillo, paesano: comprende una manciata di case, la chiesa di San Miniato e la villa che, con i suoi curatissimi giardini, sul finire del XVI secolo sostituì l'originaria fortezza. Gli interni della villa sono di un'eleganza a un tempo rustica e di gusto. Solo di recente sono stati completati i lavori per i nuovi impianti di vinificazione della tenuta, modernissimi sia sotto il profilo ecologico che sotto quello enologico.

Filippo Mazzei, Margrave Lapo Mazzei and Francesco Mazzei *(left to right)*

Filippo Mazzei, Markgraf Lapo Mazzei und Francesco Mazzei *(von links nach rechts)*

Filippo Mazzei, Marquis Lapo Mazzei et Francesco Mazzei *(de gauche à droite)*

Filippo Mazzei, Marqués Lapo Mazzei y Francesco Mazzei *(de izquierda a derecha)*

Filippo Mazzei, il marchese Lapo Mazzei e Francesco Mazzei *(da sinistra a destra)*

Located below this winery with its fabulous gardens are the new cellars, whose construction is based on a design by architect Agnese Mazzei.

Unterhalb des Weingutes mit seinen traumhaften Gärten liegen die neuen Kelleranlagen, die nach einem Entwurf der Architektin Agnese Mazzei errichtet wurden.

La nouvelle cave du domaine, construite sur un projet de l'architecte Agnese Mazzei, se situe au bas du domaine, avec ses merveilleux jardins.

Bajo las bodegas y sus fabulosos jardines se encuentran las nuevas instalaciones, realizadas según los planos de la arquitecta Agnese Mazzei.

Ai piedi della tenuta, con i suoi giardini da sogno, si trovano le nuove cantine, realizzate secondo il progetto dell'architetta Agnese Mazzei.

Castello di Meleto

Chianti, Italy

The Castello di Meleto is located at the end of a strikingly beautiful alley bordered by cypresses and juniper trees. Initially, the Castello belonged to the Benedictine monks of Coltibuono, until it came under the ownership of the Rainerii de Ricasoli family in the 13th Century. Today, its gorgeous historic rooms and ballrooms, which even include a small theater from the 18th Century, are also open to holiday guests and events. The winery estate belonging to the Castello cultivates 445 acres of vineyards and has an annual production of about 350,000 bottles.

Am Ende einer traumhaft schönen, von Zypressen und Wacholderbäumen gesäumten Allee liegt das Castello di Meleto. Das Castello gehörte zunächst den Benediktinermönchen von Coltibuono, bis es im 13. Jahrhundert in den Besitz der Familie Rainerii de Ricasoli überging. Die prachtvollen historischen Zimmer und Säle, zu denen sogar ein kleines Theater aus dem 18. Jahrhundert gehört, stehen heute auch für Feriengäste und Veranstaltungen zur Verfügung. Das zum Castello gehörende Weingut bewirtschaftet 180 ha Anbaufläche und hat eine Jahresproduktion von rund 350.000 Flaschen.

Le Castello di Meleto surgit au bout d'une merveilleuse allée bordée de cyprès et de genévriers. Il appartint d'abord aux moines bénédictins de l'abbaye de Coltibuono, avant de devenir au 13ème siècle la propriété de la famille Rainerii de Ricasoli. Les chambres et les salles historiques somptueuses, qui comprennent même un petit théâtre datant du 18ème siècle, accueillent aujourd'hui vacanciers et manifestations diverses. Le domaine viticole attenant au château exploite 180 hectares de vignes et produit annuellement quelque 350 000 bouteilles.

Un paseo custodiado por enebros y hermosos cipreses abre las puertas al Castello di Meleto. El Castello perteneció en principio a los monjes benedictinos de Coltibuono, hasta convertirse en propiedad de la familia Rainerii de Ricasoli en el siglo XIII. Hoy, las lujosas estancias y salones históricos, a los que incluso pertenece un pequeño teatro del siglo XVIII, alojan a huéspedes y se prestan a eventos. La propiedad vitícola perteneciente al Castello cultiva 180 hectáreas y cuenta con una producción anual de 350.000 botellas.

Al termine di un viale da sogno, spalleggiato da cipressi e ginepri, si erge il Castello di Meleto. Dapprima appartenente ai monaci benedettini di Coltibuono, nel XIII secolo divenne proprietà della famiglia Rainerii de Ricasoli. Oggi le magnifiche, antiche stanze e sale, tra cui si trova addirittura un piccolo teatro settecentesco, sono attrezzate anche per ospitare turisti o eventi di vario genere. L'azienda vinicola annessa al Castello cura la coltivazione di 180 ettari di vigneto e ha una produzione annua di circa 350.000 bottiglie.

Dr Roberto Garcea,
General Manager of Castello di Meleto

Dr. Roberto Garcea,
Geschäftsführer von Castello di Meleto

Dr Roberto Garcea,
Directeur Général de Castello di Meleto

Dr. Roberto Garcea,
director gerente de Castello di Meleto

Dr. Roberto Garcea,
amministratore delegato di Castello di Meleto

The unyielding fortification walls conceal the luxurious and symbolic interior of the Castello, adorned with frescos.

Hinter den trutzigen Festungsmauern verbergen sich die großzügigen und repräsentativen, mit Fresken ausgestatten Innenräume des Castellos.

A l'intérieur des murs de la forteresse se cachent les pièces du château, très spacieuses, représentatives et décorées de fresques.

Tras las sólidas murallas de la fortaleza se esconden las generosas y representativas salas pintadas con frescos.

Dietro alle possenti mura da fortezza si aprono le ricche sale di rappresentanza del Castello, decorate con affreschi.

Castello di Nipozzano

Chianti, Italy

Not far from the main part of the Chianti region, you can find the Castello di Nipozzano. The path leading up to the winery estate, which is located on a range of hills, alone, is breathtaking. It is owned by the highly traditional aristocratic Florentine Marchesi de' Frescobaldi family, which has had a close connection to Tuscan wine cultivation since the 14th Century. The family owns several properties in the vicinity of Florence, of which the Castello di Nipozzano is the most significant. Today, the wide-ranging complex that includes fortification structures, the villa from the year 1450 and the wine cellars invite wine tourists for tours, wine tasting and lodging.

Etwas abseits vom Kerngebiet des Chianti liegt das Castello di Nipozzano. Traumhaft schön ist schon der Weg zum dem auf einer Hügelkette gelegenen Weingut. Das Gut ist im Besitz des traditionsreichen florentinischen Adelsgeschlechts der Marchesi de' Frescobaldi, das seit dem 14. Jahrhundert eng mit dem Weinbau in der Toskana verbunden ist. Die Familie besitzt mehrere Güter in der Umgebung von Florenz, von denen das Castello di Nipozzano das bedeutendste ist. Der weitläufige Komplex aus Festungsanlagen, der um 1450 erbauten Villa und den Weinkellern lädt heute Weintouristen zu Besichtigungen, Verkostungen und Übernachtungen ein.

Le Castello di Nipozzano se situe un peu à l'écart du Chianti central. La route qui mène au domaine perché sur une chaîne de collines est enchanteresse. Le domaine appartient à la vieille lignée de noblesse florentine des Marchesi de' Frescobaldi, qui est étroitement liée à la culture de la vigne en Toscane depuis le 14ème siècle. La famille possède plusieurs propriétés dans les environs de Florence, et le Castello di Nipozzano est la plus importante. Le complexe très étendu, comprenant les fortifications, la villa construite en 1450 et les caves à vin, organise visites, dégustations et hébergements dans le cadre du tourisme œnologique.

El Castello di Nipozzano se ubica en un entorno algo apartado de la zona central de Chianti. Ya el camino hacia la propiedad, levantada sobre una cadena de colinas, resulta espectacular. Las bodegas son propiedad de los Marquéses de' Frescobaldi, familia noble de larga tradición y estrechamente vinculada a la producción vitivinícola en la Toscana desde el siglo XIV. La familia es dueña de diversas propiedades ubicadas en torno a Florencia, de las cuales el Castello di Nipozzano es la más significativa. El vasto complejo que comprende una fortaleza, una mansión construida en 1450 y las bodegas ofrece hoy a los turistas vinícolas visitas, catas y alojamiento.

Il Castello di Nipozzano si trova un po' in disparte rispetto all'area centrale del Chianti. Già la via che si arrampica verso la tenuta, situata su una catena di colli, è di una bellezza da sogno. La tenuta è proprietà dell'antica, nobile famiglia fiorentina dei Marchesi de' Frescobaldi, che sin dal XIV secolo è legata a doppio filo con la viticoltura toscana: tra i molti possedimenti terrieri della famiglia nei dintorni di Firenze, il Castello di Nipozzano è senz'altro il più significativo. L'ampio complesso, comprendente impianti di fortificazione, la villa costruita nel 1450 e le cantine vinicole, invita oggi gli appassionati di vino a visitare la tenuta, degustarne i prodotti e pernottare.

The Frescobaldi-family, owners of Castello di Nipozzano (among other estates)

Die Familie Frescobaldi, unter anderem Eigentümer des Castello di Nipozzano

La famille Frescobaldi, propriétaire entre autres du Castello di Nipozzano

La familia Frescobaldi, propietarios de Castello di Nipozzano, entre otros

La famiglia Frescobaldi, proprietaria di varie tenute tra cui il Castello di Nipozzano

It takes a particularly good vintage to produce a Riserva here, which first matures in Barriques for six months, then in a large wooden barrel for 16 months and finally in the bottle for about eight months before reaching the market.

Nur in besonders guten Jahren wird hier ein Riserva produziert, der zunächst sechs Monate in Barriques, dann 16 Monate im großen Holzfass und zuletzt etwa acht Monate auf der Flasche reift, bevor er in den Handel gelangt.

Ici, la « Riserva » n'est produite que les années particulièrement bonnes. Ce vin mûrit d'abord six mois en barriques, puis 16 mois dans un grand fût de bois et enfin quelque huit mois couché en bouteille, avant d'être mis en vente.

Aquí sólo se elabora un "Riserva" en años especialmente buenos. El vino se cría seis meses en barricas, más tarde 16 meses en grandes cubas de madera y los últimos ocho meses madura en botella, antes de ser comercializado.

Solo in annate particolarmente buone qui si produce un Riserva che prima di essere messo in vendita matura sei mesi in barrique, quindi 16 mesi in una grande botte di legno, per poi essere affinato circa otto mesi in bottiglia.

Rural indigenousness and their almost 700-year-old history characterize the majestic structures of the Castello di Nipozzano.

Rustikale Bodenständigkeit und eine fast 700-jährige Geschichte prägen die herrschaftlichen Gebäude des Castello di Nipozzano.

Ce qui caractérise les bâtiments seigneuriaux du Castello di Nipozzano, c'est leur profond enracinement dans leur terroir, auréolé de presque 700 ans d'histoire.

El carácter autóctono y los casi 700 años de historia se imprimen en los edificios señoriales del Castello di Nipozzano.

I signorili edifici del Castello di Nipozzano, nella loro rustica semplicità, raccontano una storia lunga quasi settecento anni.

Castello di Querceto
Chianti, Italy

The Castello di Querceto is located in a range of hills at an elevation of about 1,540 feet and is surrounded by the green of lush forests. Although there used to be a fort at this location during Roman times, today's structures were essentially established in the 16th Century. Wine cultivation is actually a fairly new tradition in these parts: It started in 1897 with a purchase made by Carlo François, who turned the country residence into a winery estate. Today, Querceto is listed among the significant and highly praised producers in the region.

Das Castello di Querceto liegt in einer Hügellandschaft auf rund 470 m Höhe, eingerahmt vom Grün üppiger Wälder. Zwar befand sich schon in römischer Zeit an dieser Stelle eine Befestigungsanlage – die heutigen Bauten sind jedoch im Wesentlichen im 16. Jahrhundert entstanden. Der Weinbau hat hier eine relativ junge Tradition: Er begann 1897 mit dem Kauf durch Carlo François, der das Landhaus in ein Weingut umwandelte. Heute zählt Querceto zu den bedeutenden und hochgeschätzten Produzenten der Region.

Le Castello di Querceto se situe dans un paysage vallonné à une hauteur d'environ 470 m, dans un écrin de forêts verdoyantes. Même si, dès l'époque romaine, il y avait une forteresse à cet endroit, les bâtiments actuels furent pour l'essentiel construits au 16ème siècle. Ici, la culture de la vigne est de tradition relativement récente : elle commença en 1897 quand Carlo François acheta la maison de campagne et la transforma en domaine viticole. Aujourd'hui, Querceto compte parmi les producteurs les plus importants et les plus estimés de la région.

El Castello di Querceto está ubicado en un paisaje de colinas a 470 m de altitud, rodeado de verdes y frondosos bosques. Si bien ya en el periodo romano en este lugar existió una fortaleza, la construcción actual data del siglo XVI. Aquí la producción vinícola es relativamente reciente: comenzó en 1897, momento en el que Carlo François compró el terreno y transformó la casa de campo en una bodega. Hoy a Querceto se le considera uno de productores significativos y apreciados de la región.

Il Castello di Querceto sorge in un paesaggio collinoso a circa 470 metri d'altezza, incorniciato del verde di folti boschi. Anche se qui già in epoca romana si trovava una struttura di fortificazione, gli edifici attuali risalgono sostanzialmente al XVI secolo. La viticoltura ha qui una tradizione relativamente giovane, in quanto ebbe inizio solo nel 1897, quando Carlo François acquistò la residenza di campagna trasformandola in una tenuta vinicola. Oggi Querceto è uno degli importanti e stimati produttori di vino della regione.

Maria Antonietta and Alessandro François, owners of *Castello di Querceto*

Maria Antonietta und Alessandro François, Eigentümer von *Castello di Querceto*

Maria Antonietta et Alessandro François, propriétaires du *Castello di Querceto*

Maria Antonietta y Alessandro François, propietarios de *Castello di Querceto*

Maria Antonietta e Alessandro François, proprietari di *Castello di Querceto*

The maturity cellars of this winery estate are located directly underneath the Castello. They are used for storing Barrique barrels with a total capacity of about 1,500 hectoliters.

Die Reifekeller des Weinguts liegen unmittelbar unter dem Castello. Dort lagern Barrique-Fässer mit einer Kapazität von insgesamt etwa 1.500 Hektolitern.

La cave de maturation du domaine se situe juste en bas du Castello. Elle abrite des barriques en chêne d'une capacité d'environ 1500 hectolitres en tout.

Las salas de crianza de la propiedad están ubicadas justo debajo del Castello. En ellas se almacenan las barricas, que en total tienen una capacidad de 1.500 hectolitros.

Le cantine d'invecchiamento della tenuta si trovano direttamente sotto il Castello: qui si conservano botti barrique per una capienza complessiva di circa 1.500 ettolitri.

The furnishings of the private living quarters of the François family also stand out with their grace and warmth.

Ebenso geschmack- wie liebevoll eingerichtet präsentieren sich die privaten Wohnräume der Familie François.

Les appartements privés de la famille François sont aménagés avec autant de goût que de charme.

También las estancias privadas de la familia François están decoradas con gusto y encanto.

L'arredamento degli appartamenti privati della famiglia François rivela la cura per il dettaglio ed il buon gusto dei proprietari.

Castello di Verrazzano

Chianti, Italy

High above the Greve Valley in the heart of the Chianti region, you can find the Castello di Verrazzano. The tradition of the Verrazzano family of growing wine and olives dates back to the 7th Century. Its most famous scion is Giovanni da Verrazzano, who explored the East Coast of America in 1524, discovering, among others, the Bay of New York and the Hudson River. Today, the Castello belongs to the Cappellini family, which cultivates the great tradition of the winery and has transformed it into one of the best wineries for Chianti Classico.

Hoch über dem Greve-Tal im Herzen des Chianti liegt das Castello di Verrazzano. Die Tradition des Wein- und Olivenanbaus an diesem Ort durch die Familie Verrazzano geht bis in das 7. Jahrhundert zurück. Ihr berühmtester Spross ist Giovanni da Verrazzano, der 1524 die Ostküste Amerikas erkundete und unter anderem die New York Bay und den Hudson River entdeckte. Heute gehört das Castello der Familie Cappellini, die die große Tradition des Weingutes pflegt und dieses in eine Spitzenkellerei für Chianti Classico verwandelt hat.

Le Castello di Verrazzano domine la vallée de Greve, au cœur du Chianti. La tradition de la culture de la vigne et de l'olivier à cet endroit, entretenue par la famille Verrazzano, remonte jusqu'au 7ème siècle. Leur descendant le plus célèbre est Giovanni da Verrazzano qui explora la côte est de l'Amérique en 1524 et découvrit, entre autres, la baie de New York et la rivière Hudson. Le Castello appartient aujourd'hui à la famille Cappellini, qui perpétue la grande tradition vinicole du domaine, devenu désormais une cave exceptionnelle pour le Chianti Classico.

Castello di Verrazzano se encuentra sobre del valle de Greve, en el corazón de Chianti. En este lugar la tradición en la producción de vino y aceitunas llevada por la familia Verrazzano se remonta hasta el siglo VII. Su vástago más famoso fue Giovanni da Verrazzano, que en 1524 exploró la costa Oeste de Estados Unidos y descubrió, entre otros lugares, la Bahía de Nueva York y el río Hudson. En la actualidad el Castello pertenece a la familia Cappellini, quien se encarga de cuidar la gran tradición de la propiedad vitícola y la ha convertido en una bodega de élite en la producción de Chianti Classico.

Alto sulla valle del Greve, nel cuore del Chianti, si erge il Castello di Verrazzano. Qui fin dal VII secolo la famiglia Verrazzano praticò la coltivazione del vino e dell'ulivo: il loro discendente più celebre è Giovanni da Verrazzano, che nel 1524 esplorò la costa orientale dell'America e scoprì tra l'altro la Baia di New York e il fiume Hudson. Oggi il castello appartiene alla famiglia Cappellini, che proseguendo la grande tradizione della tenuta l'ha trasformata in una delle migliori cantine produttrici di Chianti Classico.

Luigi Cappellini, owner of Castello di Verrazzano, together with his wife and their two daughters

Luigi Cappellini, Eigentümer von Castello di Verrazzano, zusammen mit seiner Frau und ihren beiden Töchtern

Luigi Cappellini, propriétaire du Castello di Verrazzano, avec sa femme et leurs deux filles

Luigi Cappellini, propietario de Castello di Verrazzano, junto a su esposa y sus dos hijas

Luigi Cappellini, proprietario di Castello di Verrazzano, insieme alla moglie e alle due figlie

The historic wine cellars with their rarities are open to tours and subsequent wine tasting—
"by appointment."

Die historischen Weinkeller mit ihren Raritäten stehen – nach vorheriger Anmeldung – für Besichtigungen
mit anschließender Weinprobe offen.

Les caves historiques avec leurs raretés sont ouvertes aux visites, sur réservation préalable, avec dégustation
à l'issue de la visite.

Las bodegas históricas y sus curiosidades están abiertas a visitas y cata, con previa cita.

Le storiche cantine e il loro ricco tesoro di rarità sono visitabili su appuntamento, con annessa
degustazione di vini.

Altesino

Montalcino, Italy

Palazzo Altesi—located between the hills east of Montalcino—was erected by the Tricerchi family of Tuscany in the 14th Century. For many decades, Altesino has been understood to be the pioneer in wine cultivation as well as marketing: It was here that the first Grappa di Fattoria was offered in 1977, that French Barrique barrels were used for the first time in the Montalcino region and, in 1985, that the Brunello was sold in advance in the form of "futures." Altesino has been under the ownership of Signora Elisabetta Gnudi Angelini since the year 2002.

Der Palazzo Altesi – zwischen den Hügeln östlich von Montalcino gelegen – wurde im 14. Jahrhundert von der toskanischen Familie Tricerchi errichtet. Seit vielen Jahrzehnten versteht sich Altesino als Pionier des Weinanbaus und der Vermarktung: Hier wurde 1977 der erste Grappa di Fattoria angeboten, erstmals im Montalcino-Gebiet wurden hier französische Barriques verwendet und 1985 verkaufte Altesino zum ersten Mal Brunello vorab in Form von „Futures". Seit dem Jahre 2002 befindet sich Altesino im Besitz von Signora Elisabetta Gnudi Angelini.

Le Palazzo Altesi – situé au milieu des collines à l'est de Montalcino – fut édifié au 14ème siècle par la famille toscane Tricerchi. Depuis plusieurs décennies, Altesino se veut le pionnier de la viticulture et de la commercialisation : c'est ici que fut lancé en 1977 le premier Grappa di Fattoria, que furent utilisées des barriques françaises pour la première fois dans la région de Montalcino, et que fut vendu le Brunello en 1985 au préalable sous forme de « Futures ». Depuis 2002, Altesino appartient à la Signora Elisabetta Gnudi Angelini.

El Palazzo Altesi, ubicado entre colinas al este de Montalcino, fue erigido en el siglo XIV por la familia toscana Tricerchi. Desde hace décadas Altesino figura como el pionero de la producción y comercialización de vino. Fue aquí donde en 1977 se produjo la primera Grappa di Fattoria, donde por primera vez en la zona de Montalcino se utilizaron barricas francesas y donde en 1985 se vendió Brunello en forma de futuros de bolsa. Desde el año 2002 el dominio pertenece a la Signora Elisabetta Gnudi Angelini.

Il Palazzo Altesi, situato tra le colline a est di Montalcino, fu fatto erigere nel XIV secolo dalla famiglia toscana dei Tricerchi. Da molti decenni Altesino svolge un'azione pionieristica nel settore vitivinicolo e della commercializzazione: qui fu ideata la prima Grappa di Fattoria, qui si utilizzarono per la prima volta nell'area di Montalcino barrique francesi e sempre qui nel 1985 furono venduti per la prima volta bottiglie di Brunello "in anteprima", sotto forma di certificati "futures". Dal 2002 la tenuta è proprietà di Elisabetta Gnudi Angelini.

Elisabetta Gnudi Angelini,
owner of Altesino

Elisabetta Gnudi Angelini,
Eigentümerin von Altesino

Elisabetta Gnudi Angelini,
propriétaire d'Altesino

Elisabetta Gnudi Angelini,
propietaria de Altesino

Elisabetta Gnudi Angelini,
proprietaria di Altesino

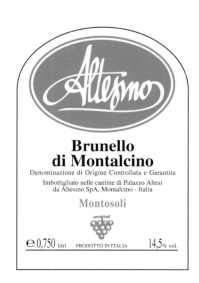

Brunello di Montalcino
Denominazione di Origine Controllata e Garantita
Imbottigliato nelle cantine di Palazzo Altesi
da Altesino SpA, Montalcino - Italia

Montosoli

e 0,750 litri   PRODOTTO IN ITALIA   14,5% vol.

Its interior is characterized by genteel restraint and simple elegance. Its cellars are used to store the "Montosoli," one of the few Brunello wines made from the grapes of one single vineyard.

Vornehme Zurückhaltung und schlichte Eleganz prägen die Innenräume. In den Kellern lagert mit dem „Montosoli" einer der wenigen Brunello-Weine, der aus Trauben einer einzigen Lage hergestellt wird.

Les intérieurs sont empreints d'une distinction discrète et d'une élégance naturelle. Dans les caves, on conserve le « Montosoli », un des rares Brunello qui soit produit avec le raisin d'une seule parcelle.

Los interiores irradian un distinguido recato y sobria elegancia. En las bodegas, con el "Montosoli" se almacena uno de los pocos vinos Brunello obtenido a partir de uvas recolectadas en un único emplazamiento.

Distinta riservatezza e sobria eleganza danno il tono agli interni. Nelle cantine, con il "Montosoli" invecchia uno dei pochi vini di Brunello che venga prodotto da uve di un unico vigneto.

Castello Banfi

Montalcino, Italy

The Banfi winery has a short but unusual history: Founded just 30 years ago, it is considered to be one of the best winery estates of Italy. With their goal to produce wine on a scale hitherto unheard of in Italy, American wine importers Harry and John Mariani acquired vast acreage in the 1980s and turned it into vineyards. In 1984, they also bought the historic Castello Poggio alle Mura from the 11th Century and gave it its present name—Castello Banfi.

Das Weingut Banfi hat eine kurze, aber außergewöhnliche Geschichte: Erst vor rund 30 Jahren gegründet, gilt es heute als eines der besten Weingüter Italiens. Mit dem Ziel, in einem bis dahin in Italien unbekannten Maßstab Wein zu produzieren, erwarben die amerikanischen Weinimporteure Harry und John Mariani in den 80er-Jahren riesige Ackerflächen und verwandelten sie in Weinberge. 1984 kauften sie zudem das historische Castello Poggio alle Mura aus dem 11. Jahrhundert und gaben ihm seinen heutigen Namen, Castello Banfi.

L'histoire du domaine de Banfi est courte mais prodigieuse : fondé il y a seulement presque 30 ans, il est considéré aujourd'hui comme l'un des meilleurs domaines viticoles d'Italie. Les importateurs de vin américains, Harry et John Mariani, achetèrent dans les années 80, d'immenses surfaces agraires qu'ils transformèrent en vignobles, avec pour objectif de produire du vin à une échelle jusqu'à présent inédite en Italie. En outre, ils acquièrent en 1984 l'historique Castello Poggio alle Mura, datant du 11ème siècle, et lui attribuèrent son nom actuel, Castello Banfi.

Las bodegas Banfi cuentan con una historia breve pero curiosa: se fundaron no hace más de 30 años y se consideran hoy una de las mejores de Italia. Con el objetivo de producir vino de primera calidad a escala, hasta entonces jamás intentado en Italia, los importadores americanos Harry y John Mariani adquirieron el enorme terreno en los años 80 y lo convirtieron en viñedo. En 1984 compraron además el histórico Castello Poggio alle Mura, erigido en el siglo XI, y le dieron su nombre actual: Castello Banfi.

L'azienda vinicola Banfi ha una storia breve, ma insolita: fondata solo una trentina d'anni fa è considerata oggi una delle migliori tenute vinicole italiane. Con l'idea di produrre vino in una scala fino ad allora ignota in Italia, negli anni Ottanta gli americani Harry e John Mariani, importatori di vini, acquistarono enormi appezzamenti agricoli per poi trasformarli in vigneti: infine nel 1984 coronarono l'opera con l'acquisto dell'antico Castello Poggio alle Mura, dell'XI secolo, che ribattezzarono Castello Banfi.

Cristina Mariani-May,
proprietor of Castello Banfi

Cristina Mariani-May,
Eigentümerin des Castello Banfi

Cristina Mariani-May,
propriétaire du Castello Banfi

Cristina Mariani-May,
propietaria de Castello Banfi

Cristina Mariani-May,
proprietaria di Castello Banfi

The swimming pool belongs to the stone houses—called "Il Borgo"—below the Castello, which have been fitted with rooms and suites for holiday guests.

Der Swimmingpool gehört zu den „Il Borgo" genannten Steinhäusern unterhalb des Castellos, in denen Zimmer und Suiten für Feriengäste eingerichtet wurden.

La piscine fait partie du groupe de maisons de pierre appelé « Il Borgo », en bas du château, dans lesquelles des chambres et des suites ont été aménagées pour les vacanciers.

La piscina pertenece a "Il Borgo", conjunto de casas de piedra ubicadas bajo el Castello, en las que se han concebido habitaciones y suites para huéspedes.

La piscina fa parte del complesso di case in pietra ai piedi del Castello, denominato "Il Borgo", in cui si trovano camere e suite per gli ospiti della tenuta.

Ciacci Piccolomini d'Aragona

Montalcino, Italy

Originally, the vineyards of Tenuta Ciacci Piccolomini d'Aragona didn't comprise more than 10 acres. It was Giuseppe Bianchini, who took over the business from the ownership of the Ciacci and Piccolomini families in 1985, expanded the vineyards into about 100 acres and set up a modern production facility. Today, Giuseppe's children, Paolo and Lucia Bianchini, manage the winery. The heart of the estate is and remains the magnificent renaissance palace from the 17th Century in the town of Castelnuovo dell'Abate.

Die Anbaufläche der Tenuta Ciacci Piccolomini d'Aragona umfasste ursprünglich nicht mehr als vier Hektar. Erst Giuseppe Bianchini, der 1985 den Betrieb aus dem Besitz der Familien Ciacci und Piccolomini übernahm, erweiterte die Rebflächen auf ca. 40 ha und errichtete ein modernes Produktionsgebäude. Heute wird das Weingut von Giuseppes Kindern Paolo und Lucia Bianchini geführt. Herzstück des Betriebs ist nach wie vor der prachtvolle, aus dem 17. Jahrhundert stammende Renaissance-palast im Ort Castelnuovo dell'Abate.

Le vignoble de la Tenuta Ciacci Piccolomini d'Aragona ne comptait à l'origine pas plus de quatre hectares. C'est seulement Giuseppe Bianchini qui, ayant repris l'ex-ploitation en 1985 sur la propriété des familles Ciacci et Piccolomini, agrandit le vignoble sur quelque 40 hectares et fit construire une cuverie moderne. Aujourd'hui, les enfants de Giuseppe, Paolo et Lucia Bianchini, dirigent le domaine. Le cœur de l'exploitation reste le somptueux palais Renaissance qui date du 17ème siècle, dans la commune de Castelnuovo dell'Abate.

En origen la superficie de cultivo de Tenuta Ciacci Piccolomini d'Aragona no abarcaba más de cuatro hectáreas. Fue Giuseppe Bianchini quien, en 1985, adquirió la propiedad de las familias Ciacci y Piccolomini, amplió los viñedos en 40 hectáreas y construyó un moderno edificio de producción. Hoy dirigen las bodegas los hijos de Giuseppe, Paolo y Lucia Bianchini. El alma de la empresa sigue siendo el exuberante palacio de estilo renacentista del siglo XVII ubicado en Castelnuovo dell'Abate.

Originariamente la superficie coltivata a vigneto nella Tenuta Ciacci Piccolomini d'Aragona non superava i quattro ettari. Solo dal 1985, quando Giuseppe Bianchini è subentrato alle famiglie Ciacci e Piccolomini nella guida dell'azienda, i vigneti sono stati ampliati fino a raggiungere i 40 ettari di superficie ed è stata costruita una mo-derna cantina di vinificazione. Attualmente a capo della tenuta ci sono i due figli di Giuseppe, Paolo e Lucia Bianchini. Oggi come allora il cuore della tenuta è il magnifico palazzo rinascimentale del Seicento, situato in località Castelnuovo dell'Abate.

Paolo and Lucia Bianchini,
owners of Ciacci Piccolomini d'Aragona

Paolo und Lucia Bianchini,
Eigentümer von Ciacci Piccolomini d'Aragona

Paolo et Lucia Bianchini,
propriétaires de Ciacci Piccolomini d'Aragona

Paolo y Lucia Bianchini,
propietarios de Ciacci Piccolomini d'Aragona

Paolo e Lucia Bianchini,
proprietari di Ciacci Piccolomini d'Aragona

Fabius de'Vecchis, *Abbot of Sant'Antimo and the Bishop of Montalcino, had this typically Tuscan Palazzo erected in 1672. Today, it houses the wine trade of the estate.*

Fabius de'Vecchis, *Abt von Sant'Antimo und Bischof von Montalcino, ließ 1672 den typisch toskanischen Palazzo errichten, in dem heute der Weinverkauf des Gutes untergebracht ist.*

Fabius de'Vecchis, *abbé de Sant'Antimo et évêque de Montalcino, fit construire en 1672 ce palais toscan typique qui abrite aujourd'hui l'espace de vente des vins du domaine.*

En 1672, Fabius de'Vecchis, *abad de Sant'Antimo y obispo de Montalcino, hizo construir un típico palazzo toscano, en el que actualmente se realiza la venta de los vinos de la propiedad.*

Nel 1672 Fabius de'Vecchis, *abate di Sant'Antimo e vescovo di Montalcino, diede incarico di costruire il palazzo dallo stile tipicamente toscano in cui oggi si vendono i vini della tenuta.*

Vergelegen
Cape Winelands, South Africa

The farm fields of Vergelegen comprise more than 7,413 acres, 259 of which are cultivated as vineyards. Wine cultivation in this area dates back to the year 1700, which makes Vergelegen one of the oldest wineries on the Cape. Abandoned at times, it was not revived until 1987 after being purchased by Anglo-American Farms Ltd. Even though the winery is located in one of the coolest regions of the country, late vintage and cutting-edge cellar technology produce excellent quality. The historic farm manor, the library and the idyllic gardens of Vergelegen are open to guests and visitors.

Das Farmgelände von Vergelegen umfasst über 3.000 ha, von denen 105 als Rebflächen kultiviert sind. Der Weinbau an dieser Stelle geht bis auf das Jahr 1700 zurück – damit ist Vergelegen eines der ältesten Weingüter am Kap. Zwischenzeitlich aufgegeben, wurde es erst 1987 nach dem Kauf durch die Anglo-American Farms Ltd. wieder belebt. Obwohl das Gut in einer der kühlsten Gegenden des Landes gelegen ist, sorgen späte Lese und modernste Kellertechnik für eine exzellente Qualität. Das historische Gutshaus, die Bibliothek und die idyllischen Gärten von Vergelegen stehen Gästen und Besuchern offen.

L'exploitation de Vergelegen couvre plus de 3000 hectares, dont 105 consacrés aux vignes. La viticulture à cet endroit remonte à l'année 1700 – Vergelegen est donc le plus ancien domaine viticole du Cap. Abandonné entre-temps, il n'a retrouvé son activité qu'en 1987, date à laquelle la société Anglo-American Farms Ltd. l'acheta. Bien que le domaine soit situé dans l'une des régions les plus fraîches du pays, des vendanges tardives et des techniques de vinification ultramodernes assurent une excellente qualité. Le manoir historique, la bibliothèque et les jardins idylliques de Vergelegen accueillent les hôtes et les visiteurs.

El recinto de la granja Vergelegen abarca más de 3.000 hectáreas, en 105 de las cuales se cultivan cepas. La producción de vino de este lugar se remonta al año 1700, lo que convierte a Vergelegen en uno de los dominios vitícolas más antiguos del Cabo. Tras abandonarse entre tanto, en 1987 se volvió a poner en funcionamiento, al ser adquirido por Anglo-American Farms Ltd. A pesar de estar ubicado en una de las zonas más frías del país, las cosechas tardías y la más moderna técnica bodeguera se encargan de potenciar una excelente calidad. La mansión histórica, la biblioteca y los idílicos jardines de Vergelegen están abiertos al público.

Il territorio della farm di Vergelegen comprende oltre 3.000 ettari, di cui 105 coltivati a vigneto. Dal momento che qui la viticoltura ha una tradizione risalente al 1700, Vergelegen è una delle più antiche aziende vinicole sul Capo. Dopo una fase di abbandono, solo nel 1987 la tenuta è stata riattivata da un nuovo proprietario, la Anglo-American Farms Ltd. Nonostante ci si trovi qui in una delle regioni più fredde del Sudafrica, una vendemmia tardiva e l'utilizzo di modernissime tecniche di vinificazione consentono di raggiungere una qualità eccellente. La dimora storica, la biblioteca e gli idillici giardini di Vergelegen sono aperti ad ospiti e visitatori.

Don Tooth, *Managing Director of Vergelegen and Cynthia Carroll, CEO of Anglo American plc – the parent company of the winery*

Don Tooth, *Geschäftsführer von Vergelegen, und Cynthia Carroll, Generaldirektorin von Anglo American plc – der Muttergesellschaft des Weingutes*

Don Tooth, *Gérant de Vergelegen, et Cynthia Carroll, Directeur Général d'Anglo American plc – la maison mère du domaine*

Don Tooth, *director gerente de Vergelegen y Cynthia Carroll, directora de Anglo American plc, compañía matriz de las bodegas*

Don Tooth, *amministratore delegato di Vergelegen, e Cynthia Carroll, direttrice generale di Anglo American plc – società madre dell'azienda vinicola*

1993 saw the completion of the winery's new production facility. Underneath the ground level are three cellar levels in which the vinification takes place based on the principle of "gravity flow."

1993 wurde das neue Produktionsgebäude des Weingutes errichtet. Unter einem oberirdischen Geschoss liegen drei Kellergeschosse, in denen die Vinifikation nach dem Prinzip des „gravity flow" durchgeführt wird.

Les nouvelles installations de production du domaine ont été construites en 1993. Le rez-de-chaussée est en surface et il y a trois étages souterrains de cave dans lesquels la vinification se fait suivant le principe de la « gravity flow ».

En 1993 se erigió el nuevo edificio de elaboración de las bodegas. Bajo una planta a ras de tierra se encuentran tres pisos subterráneos de bodegas en las que se vinifica según el principio de "gravity flow".

Il nuovo edificio per la produzione è stato costruito nel 1993: sotto ad un piano sopraelevato si trovano ben tre piani interrati di cantine, in cui si procede alla vinificazione seguendo il principio del "gravity flow".

Even the interior of this estate, which is situated in a valley and whose garden contains the oldest oaks in South Africa, still radiates all the charm of the past centuries.

Das in einem Talkessel gelegene Gutshaus, *in dessen Garten die ältesten Eichen Südafrikas stehen, strahlt auch in seinen Innenräumen noch ganz den Charme der vergangenen Jahrhunderte aus.*

Dans le manoir, situé au fond de la vallée *et dont les jardins renferment les plus vieux chênes d'Afrique du Sud, les intérieurs possèdent encore tout le charme des siècles passés.*

La hacienda ubicada en el valle, *en cuyo un jardín crecen los robles más antiguos de Sudáfrica, irradia también en sus estancias el encanto de siglos pasados.*

Nel giardino della tenuta, situata in una conca valliva, *crescono le più antiche querce di tutto il Sudafrica. Anche negli interni si respira ancora tutto il fascino dei secoli passati.*

Graham Beck Franschhoek Estate

Cape Winelands, South Africa

Businessman Graham Beck, who made his fortune in coal mining, among other ventures, founded his own winery in 1983. With plenty of savvy, he turned this venture rapidly into a success as well. That's why Graham Beck Wines is one of the most influential, independent wine producers of South Africa. At this point, his business consists of two wineries: One in Robertson/Breederiver Valley and one in Franschhoek Valley. Franschhoek Cellar has turned out to be an especially remarkable winery building, in whose center stands a large production facility for red wines, which is lined in natural stone.

Der Geschäftsmann Graham Beck, der sein Vermögen unter anderem im Kohlebergbau gemacht hat, gründete 1983 ein eigenes Weingut. Auch dieses führte er mit viel Geschick rasch zum Erfolg: So ist Graham Beck Wines heute einer der größten unabhängigen Weinproduzenten Südafrikas. Das Unternehmen besteht inzwischen aus zwei Kellereien: eine in Robertson/Breederiver Valley und eine im Franschhoek Valley. Mit dem Franschhoek Cellar entstand dort ein besonders eindrucksvolles Gutsgebäude, in dessen Zentrum eine große, natursteinverkleidete Produktionsanlage für Rotweine steht.

L'homme d'affaires Graham Beck, qui fit fortune, entre autres, dans l'exploitation de la houille, fonda son propre domaine viticole en 1983. Là encore, grâce à sa grande habileté, l'entreprise fut rapidement une réussite : ainsi la société Graham Beck Wines est-elle aujourd'hui l'un des plus importants producteurs de vin indépendants d'Afrique du Sud. Entre-temps, l'entreprise comprend deux caves : l'une à Robertson, dans la Breederiver Valley et l'autre dans la Franschhoek Valley. On y a construit la Franschhoek Cellar, un bâtiment particulièrement imposant au centre duquel se tiennent de grandes installations de production de vin rouge au revêtement de pierre naturelle.

El hombre de negocios Graham Beck, que creó su patrimonio en parte a través de la extracción de carbón, fundó en 1983 sus propias bodegas, y las llevó al éxito con la misma rapidez y destreza. Y de este modo Graham Beck Wines es hoy uno de los mayores productores de vino independientes de Sudáfrica. Entre tanto, la empresa comprende ya dos bodegas: una de ellas en Robertson/Breederiver Valley y la otra en Franschhoek Valley. Con Franschhoek Cellar surgió un impresionante edificio, en cuyo centro se ubica una gran planta de producción de vino tinto totalmente revestida de piedra natural.

L'imprenditore Graham Beck, che doveva la sua ricchezza tra le altre cose all'attività di estrazione del carbone, nel 1983 ha fondato un'azienda vinicola propria, che ha condotto con altrettanta abilità ad un pronto successo: basti pensare che oggi Graham Beck Wines è uno dei più grandi produttori vinicoli indipendenti del Sudafrica. L'azienda ormai comprende due cantine: una a Robertson/Breederiver Valley ed una nella Franschhoek Valley. Qui, con le cantine Franschhoek Cellar, è sorto un edificio particolarmente interessante, al cui centro si trova un grande impianto di produzione per vini rossi dalle pareti ricoperte in pietra viva.

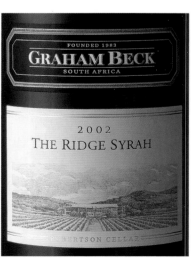

Graham Beck, owner of Franschhoek Estate, with his family

Graham Beck, Eigentümer von Franschhoek Estate, mit seiner Familie

Graham Beck, propriétaire de Franschhoek Estate, avec sa famille

Graham Beck, propietario de Franschhoek Estate, junto a su familia

Graham Beck, proprietario di Franschhoek Estate, con la famiglia

Nederburg
Cape Winelands, South Africa

German immigrant Phillipus Wolvaart founded the Nederburg winery in 1792. With an annual production of 10 million bottles, it is the largest winery estate in South Africa, producing both plain Cape Riesling wines as well as exclusive wines like the "Edelkeuer." 1% of the annual production is not destined for the free market. Instead, it can be purchased in the form of special bottles, such as "Limited Vintage" and "Private Bin" at the Nederburg wine auctions, which have been taking place there every year since 1975.

Das Weingut Nederburg wurde 1792 von dem deutschen Auswanderer Phillipus Wolvaart gegründet. Mit einer Jahresproduktion von 10 Millionen Flaschen ist es das größte Weingut Südafrikas, das sowohl einfache Cape Riesling-Weine, aber auch exklusive Tropfen wie den „Edelkeuer" produziert. 1% der Jahresproduktion gelangt nicht in den freien Handel, sondern kann in Form von Spezialabfüllungen wie „Limited Vintage" und „Private Bin" bei den seit 1975 jährlich auf Nederburg stattfindenden Weinauktionen ersteigert werden.

Le domaine de Nederburg fut fondé en 1792 par l'émigrant allemand Phillipus Wolvaart. Sa production annuelle atteint 10 millions de bouteilles et c'est donc le plus grand domaine viticole d'Afrique du Sud, produisant aussi bien de simples Riesling du Cap que d'excellents élixirs tels que l'« Edelkeuer ». 1% de la production annuelle n'est pas mis en vente libre, mais mis spécialement en bouteilles, telles que les « Limited Vintage » et « Private Bin », vendues aux enchères, une fois par an depuis 1975, au domaine de Nederburg.

Las bodegas fueron fundadas en 1792 por el alemán emigrado Phillipus Wolvaart. Con una producción de 10 millones de botellas, se ha convertido en la propiedad vitivinícola más grande de Sudáfrica y no sólo produce los vinos sencillos Cape Riesling, sino también caldos exclusivos como „Edelkeuer". El 1% de la producción anual no se vende en el mercado libre, sino como embotellados especiales del tipo "Limited Vintage" y "Private Bin", por los que, desde 1975, se puja en las subastas anuales de Nederburg.

Fondata nel 1792 dall'emigrato tedesco Phillipus Wolvaart, la tenuta di Nederburg produce oggi 10 milioni di bottiglie all'anno, dai semplici Cape-Riesling a vini eccellenti come l'"Edelkeuer", ed è pertanto la più grande azienda vitivinicola del Sudafrica. L'1% della produzione annua non arriva sul libero mercato, ma può essere acquistata solo sotto forma di edizione limitata, come per esempio "Limited Vintage" e "Private Bin", nel corso delle aste vinicole che Nederburg ospita ogni anno sin dal 1975.

*Cellar Master, **Razvan Macici**, and his assistants Tariro Masayiti (white wine) and Elunda Basson (red wine).*

*Kellermeister **Razvan Macici** und seine Assistenten Tariro Masayiti (Weißwein) und Elunda Basson (Rotwein)*

*Le caviste **Razvan Macici** et ses assistants Tariro Masayiti (vin blanc) et Elunda Basson (vin rouge)*

***Razvan Macici,** bodeguero y sus asistentes Tariro Masayiti (vino blanco) y Elunda Basson (vino tinto)*

*L'enologo **Razvan Macici** con i suoi assistenti Tariro Masayiti (vino bianco) e Elunda Basson (vino rosso)*

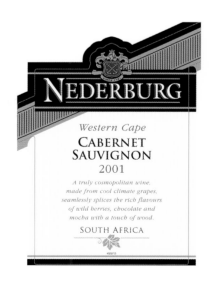

Index

USA

California

Opus One
7900 St. Helena Highway, Oakville, CA 94562, USA
T +1 707 944 9442, F +1 707 948 2497
www.opusonewinery.com, info@opusonewinery.com

Open daily 10 am to 4 pm. Tastings by appointment. Opus One offers a guided tour through winery, cellars and vineyards, including a complimentary tasting of the current vintage (by appointment).

Recommended wines: Opus One. Second wine: Overture (only available for sale at the winery)

California

Quintessa
1601 Silverado Trail, Rutherford, CA 94573, USA
T +1 707 967 1601, F +1 707 286 2727
www.quintessa.com, info@quintessa.com

Open daily 10 am to 4 pm. Hosted tastings of two vintages are available to visitors by appointment. Private guided tours offered daily by appointment at 10.30 am, 12.30 pm and 2.30 pm.

Recommended wine: Quintessa, a blend of Cabernet Sauvignon, Merlot, and Cabernet Franc

California

Rubicon Estate
1991 St. Helena Highway, Rutherford, CA 94573, USA
T +1 800 782 4266, F +1 707 967 9084
www.rubiconestate.com, info@rubiconestate.com

Open daily 10 am to 5 pm. Guided tours offered hourly between 10.30 am and 3.30 pm, special tours at 10 am, 11 am and 1 pm. Rubicon offers the "Mammarella" wine bar, a wine library and the so-called "Centennial Museum", which features artifacts from the Inglenook winery and Coppola family films.

Recommended wine: Rubicon, blended primarily from an old Cabernet Sauvignon clone, first planted on the Estate 1882

France

Bordeaux

Saint-Julien

Château Beychevelle
33250 Saint-Julien-Beychevelle, France
T +33 5 56 73 20 70, F +33 5 56 73 20 71
www.beychevelle.com, mdv@beychevelle.com

Open Monday to Friday 10 am to noon and 1.30 pm to 5 pm, Saturday in July and August. Possibility of tasting and buying wine directly at the winery. Guided cellar tours by appointment. Art exhibitions occasionally during summer.

Recommended wines: Château Beychevelle Grand Cru Classé Saint-Julien. Second wine: Amiral de Beychevelle

Saint-Julien

Château Talbot
33250 Saint-Julien-Beychevelle, France
T +33 5 56 73 21 50, F +33 5 56 73 21 51
www.chateau-talbot.com, chateau-talbot@chateau-talbot.com

Open by appointment Monday to Friday 9 am to 11 am and 2 pm to 4 pm. Cellar tours with tasting of the last vintage. No sales directly at the winery. The living quarters are private.

Recommended wines: Château Talbot Grand Cru Classé Saint-Julien. Second wine: Connétable Talbot

Margaux

Château du Tertre
14, allée du Tertre, 33460 Arsac, France
T +33 5 57 88 52 52, F +33 5 57 88 52 51
www.chateaudutertre.fr, receptif@chateaudutertre.fr

Open daily 9.30 am to 12.30 pm and 1.30 pm to 5 pm. Possibility for tasting and buying wine directly at the winery. Guided tours by appointment from Monday to Saturday. Bed & breakfast available.

Recommended wines: Château du Tertre Grand Cru Classé Margaux. Second wine: Les Hauts du Tertre

Margaux

Château Giscours
Labarde, 33460 Margaux, France
T +33 5 57 97 09 09, F +33 5 57 97 09 00
www.chateau-giscours.fr, receptif@chateau-giscours.fr

Open daily 9.30 am to 12.30 pm and 1.30 pm to 5.30 pm. Possibility for tasting and buying wine directly at the winery. Guided tours by appointment from Monday to Saturday, and every day in April and June. Bed & breakfast available.

Recommended wines: Château Giscours Grand Cru Classé Margaux. Second wine: La Sirène de Giscours

Margaux

Château Palmer
Cantenac, 33460 Margaux, France
T +33 5 57 88 72 72, F +33 5 57 88 37 16
www.chateau-palmer.com, chateau-palmer@chateau-palmer.com

Open Monday to Friday April to October 10 am to 12.30 pm and 2.15 pm to 6.30 pm, October to March 9 am to 12.30 pm and 2.15 pm to 5.30 pm. Guided tours by appointment. No tasting and sales directly at the winery.

Recommended wines: Château Palmer Grand Cru Classé Margaux. Second wine: Alter Ego

Pauillac

Château Latour
Saint-Lambert, 33250 Pauillac, France
T +33 5 56 73 19 80, F +33 5 56 73 19 81
www.chateau-latour.fr, s.favreau@chateau-latour.com

Open from Monday to Friday, 8.30 am to 12.30 pm and 2 pm to 5 pm. Possibility of tastings, no sales directly at the winery. Guided tours by appointment.

Recommended wines: Château Latour Grand Cru Classé Pauillac. Second wine: Les Forts de Latour

Pauillac

Château Pichon-Longueville
33250 Pauillac, France
T +33 5 56 73 17 17, F +33 5 56 73 17 28
www.pichonlongueville.com, contact@pichonlongueville.com

Open daily from 9 am to 12.30 pm and from 2 pm to 6.30 pm. Guided tour of the vineyards and technical facilities by appointment, tasting included. Six bedrooms for bed & breakfast. Buffet or gala luncheon by appointment. A wine shop is located at the Château.

Recommended wines: Château Pichon-Longueville Grand Cru Classé Pauillac. Second wine: Les Tourelles de Longueville

Pessac-Léognan

Château Haut-Bailly
33850 Léognan, France
T +33 5 56 64 75 11, F +33 5 56 64 53 60
www.chateau-haut-bailly.com, mail@chateau-haut-bailly.com

Visits by appointment only: Monday to Friday 9 am to noon and 2 pm to 5 pm. Guided tours through winery, cellars and vineyards, including a tasting. No sales directly at the winery. The living quarters are private.

Recommended wines: Château Haut-Bailly Grand Cru Classé Pessac-Léognan. Second wine: La Parde de Haut-Bailly

Pessac-Léognan

Château Smith Haut Lafitte
33650 Bordeaux-Martillac, France
T +33 5 57 83 11 22, F +33 5 57 83 11 21
www.smith-haut-lafitte.com, visites@smith-haut-lafitte.com

Open daily 9 am to 6 pm. Visits, tastings, sales and guided tours by appointment. Hotel Les Sources de Caudalie with 2 restaurants can be found within 110 yards (100 m) of the winery.

Recommended wines: Château Smith Haut Lafitte Grand Cru Classé de Graves. Second wine: Les Hauts de Smith

Saint-Emilion

Château Canon la Gaffeliere
Vignobles Comtes de Neipperg, 33330 Saint-Emilion, France
T +33 5 57 24 71 33, F +33 5 57 24 67 95
www.canon-la-gaffeliere.com, info@neipperg.com

Open Monday to Friday 9 am to noon and 2 pm to 5 pm. Guided tours and tastings by appointment only. No sales directly at the winery.

Recommended wine: Château Canon-la-Gaffelière Grand Cru Classé de Saint-Emilion

Saint-Emilion

Château Figeac
33330 Saint-Emilion, France
T +33 5 57 24 72 26, F +33 5 57 74 45 74
www.chateau-figeac.com, chateau-figeac@chateau-figeac.com

Open Monday to Friday by appointment only. Guided tours through the winery, including a tasting. No sales directly at the winery. The living quarters are private.

Recommended wine: Château Figeac Grand Cru Classé Saint-Emilion

Saint-Emilion

Château Pavie
Vignobles Perse, 33330 Saint-Emilion
T +33 5 57 55 43 43, F +33 5 57 24 63 99
www.chateaupavie.com, contact@vignoblesperse.com

Winery and château are not open to visitors. The Hostellerie de Plaisance guest house, situated in the heart of Saint-Emilion village, belongs to the owners of Château Pavie.

Recommended wine: Château Pavie Grand Cru Classé Saint-Emilion

Burgundy

Cote d'Or

Domaine de la Pousse d'Or
Cote d'Or, 21190 Volnay, France
T +33 3 80 21 61 33, F +33 3 80 21 29 97
www.lapoussedor.fr, secretaire@lapoussedor.fr

Visits and guided tours by appointment only. Possibility of tasting and buying wine directly at the winery. The living quarters are private.

Recommended wines: Clos de la Bousse d'Or Volnay 1er Cru - Monopole, Clos des 60 Ouvrées Volnay 1er Cru - Monopole

Cote d'Or

Louis Latour
Château Corton Grancey, Côte de Beaune, 21420 Aloxe-Corton, France
T +33 3 80 24 81 10, F +33 3 80 22 36 21
www.louislatour.com, louislatour@louislatour.com

The winery is not open to the public.

Recommended wines: Château Corton Grancey Grand Cru, Corton-Charlemagne Grand Cru

Spain

Rioja

Marqués de Riscal
01340 Elciego, Álava, Spain
T +34 945 60 60 00, F +34 945 60 60 23
www.marquesderiscal.com, marquesderiscal@marquesderiscal.com

Open daily from 10 am to 10 pm. Guided tours daily except Monday through winery and cellars must be booked in advance. Marqués de Riscal offers a wine shop, a wine restaurant and a banquet hall. A luxury hotel with restaurant and wine spa also belongs to the winery.

Recommended wines: Marqués de Riscal Reserva D.O., Barón de Chirel Reserva D.O.

Rioja

Ysios
Camino de la Hoya, s/n, 01300 Laguardia, Álava, Spain
T +34 945 60 06 40, F +34 943 44 53 02
www.bodegasysios.com, info@domecqbodegas.com

Winery tours Monday to Friday 11 am, 1 pm and 4 pm, Saturday and Sunday 11 am and 1 pm. Reservation necessary. Ysios offers a wine shop. Tastings and catering by appointment.

Recommended wine: Ysios Reserva D.O.

Aragon

Bodega Enate
Ctra. de Barbastro a Naval, km 9, 22314 Salas Bajas, Huesca, Spain
T +34 974 30 25 80, F +34 974 30 00 46
www.enate.es, bodega@enate.es

Open Monday to Friday 8.30 am to 1 pm and 3 pm to 7 pm, Saturday 9 am to 2 pm. Guided tours Monday to Friday 10 am, 11.30 am and 4.30 pm, Saturday 10 am and noon, reservation necessary. A gallery displays the original artworks used for the labels of Enate Wines.

Recommended wines: Enate Chardonnay 234 D.O., Enate Merlot D.O.

Navarra

Señorío de Otazu
31174 Echauri, Navarra, Spain
T +34 948 32 92 00, F +34 948 32 93 53
www.otazu.com, comercial@otazu.com

Open Monday to Friday 8 am to 2 pm and 3 pm to 6 pm, summer 7 am to 6 pm, visits on Saturday by appointment. Señorío de Otazu offers a wine shop. Guided tours (by appointment) include a tasting.

Recommended wines: Palacio de Otazu Dimension D.O., Palacio de Otazu Altar Reserva Especial D.O.

Navarra

Viñedos y Bodegas Señorío de Arínzano
Ctra. Estella-Tafalla, km 3, 31240 Estella, Navarra, Spain
T +34 948 81 10 00, F +34 948 81 14 07
www.bodegaschivite.com, info@bodegaschivite.com

Open Monday to Friday 9 am to 6 pm. Visits, tastings and guided tours by appointment. Private dinners can be arranged by appointment. A guest house will be opened in 2008.

Recommended wines: Chivite Colección 125 Reserva D.O., Chivite Colección 125 Chardonnay D.O.

Index

Germany

Rheingau

Weingut Robert Weil
Mühlberg 5, 65399 Kiedrich, Germany
T +49 6123 2308, F +49 6123 1546
www.weingut-robert-weil.com, info@weingut-robert-weil.com

Open Monday to Friday 8 am to 5.30 pm, Saturday 10 am to 4 pm, Sunday 11 am to 5 pm. Weingut Robert Weil offers a wine shop. Guided tours and tastings by appointment.

Recommended wines: Kiedrich Gräfenberg Erstes Gewächs, Kiedrich Gräfenberg Riesling Spätlese

Palatinate

Weingut Dr. Bürklin-Wolf
Weinstraße 65, 67157 Wachenheim, Germany
T +49 6322 9533 0, F +49 6322 9533 30
www.buerklin-wolf.de, bb@buerklin-wolf.de

Open daily 11 am to 6 pm. The winery offers a wine shop and tastings. Guided tours are by appointment. The gourmet restaurant "Bürklin's Restaurant zur Kanne" and the wine bar within Hofgut Ruppertsberg are part of Weingut Dr. Bürklin-Wolf.

Recommended wines: Pechstein Riesling GC, Kirchenstück Riesling GC

Württemberg

Weingut Fürst zu Hohenlohe-Oehringen
Im Schloß, 74613 Öhringen, Germany
From 2008: Wiesenkelter 1, 74613 Öhringen-Verrenberg
T +49 7941 94910, F +49 7941 37349
www.verrenberg.de, info@verrenberg.de

Open Monday to Friday 8 am to noon and 1 pm to 5 pm, Saturday 9 am to noon. Guided tours and tastings by appointment. A new winery with wine bar will be opened in 2008. Schloss Neuenstein, residence of Fürst zu Hohenlohe-Oehringen with a museum, is located nearby.

Recommended wines: Verrenberger Verrenberg Riesling Spätlese trocken "Butzen", EX Flammis Orior HADES red blend

Austria

Burgenland

Leo Hillinger
Hill 1, 7093 Jois, Austria
T +43 2160 8317 0, F +43 2160 8317 17
www.leo-hillinger.com, office@leo-hillinger.com

Open Monday to Friday 9 am to 6 pm, Saturday and Sunday 11 am to 6 pm. Guided tours, special events, snacks and a tasting by appointment.

Recommended wines: Hill 1, Pinot Noir

Italy

South Tyrol

Alois Lageder
IM PARADEIS
St. Gertraud Platz 5, 39040 Margreid, Italy
T +39 0471 818 080, F + 39 0471 809 550
www.aloislageder.eu, imparadeis@aloislageder.eu

Open Monday to Friday 10 am to 7 pm, Saturday 10 am to 5 pm. Alois Lageder offers a wine shop and a wine bar. Guided tours through cellars of Tòr Löwengang and vineyards by appointment. Alois Lageder regularly hosts concerts and art exhibitions.

Recommended wines: LÖWENGANG Chardonnay, COR RÖMIGBERG Cabernet Sauvignon

South Tyrol

MANINCOR
St. Josef am See 4, 39052 Kaltern, Italy
T +39 0471 960 230, F +39 0471 960 204
www.manincor.com, info@manincor.com

The wine shop (with possibility for tastings) is open Monday to Friday 9.30 am to 12.30 pm and 1 pm to 6 pm, Saturday 10 am to 2 pm. MANINCOR offers guided cellar tours (reservation necessary).

Recommended wines: Cassiano, Sophie, Moscato Giallo

Piedmont

Fontanafredda
Via Alba 15, 12050 Serralunga d'Alba, Italy
T +39 0173 626 111, F +39 0173 613 451
www.fontanafredda.it, info@fontanafredda.it

Open Monday to Friday 8.30 am to 6.30 pm. Fontanafredda offers a wine shop and a wine bar. Guided tours by appointment. Event center, restaurant and accommodation are only available by reservation.

Recommended wines: Fontanafredda Lazzarito Vigna La Delizia Barolo D.O.C.G., Moncucco Moscato d'Asti D.O.C.G.

Piedmont

Marchesi di Barolo
Via Alba 12, 12060 Barolo, Italy
T +39 0173 564 400, F +39 0173 564 444
www.marchesibarolo.com, reception@marchesibarolo.com

Open daily 10.30 am to 5.30 pm, except August. Marchesi di Barolo offers a wine shop. Guided cellar tours and tastings by appointment. The restaurant is open daily, reservation necessary. The Barolo Castle and Corkscrew Museum are open to visitors.

Recommended wines: Marchesi die Barolo Barolo Cannubi D.O.C.G., Barbera d'Alba Paiagal D.O.C.

Piedmont

Castello di Verduno
Via Umberto I/9, 12060 Verduno, Italy
T +39 0172 470 125, F +39 0172 470 298
www.castellodiverduno.com, cantina@castellodiverduno.com

Open Monday to Friday 9.30 am to 1 pm and 2.30 pm to 6 pm, Saturday 9.30 am to 1 pm. Castello di Verduno offers a wine shop. Guided cellar tours by appointment. A hotel in the old castle and a country house called "Cà del Re" in Verduno village belong to the winery. Both have a restaurant with the typical cuisine of the Langhe.

Recommended wines: Castello di Verduno Barolo Massara D.O.C.G., Verduno Basadone D.O.C.

Toscana

Chianti

Badia a Coltibuono
53013 Gaiole in Chianti, Italy
T +39 0577 744 832, F +39 0577 744 839
www.coltibuono.de, badia@coltibuono.com

Open daily 8.30 am to 6 pm. Visits and tastings Tuesday, Wednesday and Friday 11 am (by appointment). Badia a Coltibuono offers a wine shop in an old tavern house nearby, open daily April to October 9.30 am to 1 pm and 2 pm to 6.30 pm (in winter closed on Sunday and Monday morning). A restaurant with garden terrace is situated in the refurbished stables. Bed & breakfast is available in the old abbey.

Recommended wines: Badia a Coltibuono Chianti Classico Riserva D.O.C.G., Sangioveto IGT

Chianti

Barone Ricasoli
Cantine del Castello di Brolio, 53013 Gaiole in Chianti, Italy
T +39 0577 730 1, F +39 0577 730 225
www.ricasoli.it, barone@ricasoli.it

Open Monday to Friday 9 am to 7.30 pm, Saturday and Sunday 11 am to 6.30 pm (summer), Monday to Friday 9 am to 5.30 pm (winter). Barone Ricasoli offers a wine shop. Guided tours and special themed tours on various aspects of vinification by appointment. Castle's garden and chapel are open to the public.

Recommended wines: Brolio Barone Ricasoli Chianti Classico D.O.C.G., Castello di Brolio Chianti Classico D.O.C.G., Castello di Brolio Casalferro IGT

Chianti

Castello di Fonterutoli
Marchesi Mazzei SPA, Via Ottone III 5, 53011 Castellina in Chianti, Italy
T +39 0577 735 71, F +39 0577 735 757
www.fonterutoli.it, mazzei@mazzei.it

Open Monday, Tuesday and Saturday 9 am to 7 pm, Wednesday and Friday 9 am to 8 pm, Sunday 10 am to 1 pm and 2 pm to 7 pm (April to October), Monday and Saturday 9.30 am to 12.30 pm and 1.30 pm to 6.30 pm, Tuesday to Friday 9.30 am to 6.30 pm (November to March). Castello di Fonterutoli offers a wine shop and guided tours (by appointment). The Osteria di Fonterutoli restaurant offers Tuscan cuisine in an old country home. Castello di Fonterutoli provides hospitality in elegant apartments.

Recommended wines: Fonterutoli Chianti Classico D.O.C.G., Castello di Fonterutoli Chianti Classico D.O.C.G.

Chianti

Castello di Meleto
53013 Gaiole in Chianti, Italy
T +39 0577 749 217, F +39 0577 749 762
www.castellomeleto.it, info@castellomeleto.it

The wine shop is open daily during the summer season from 9 am to 7.30 pm. Guided tours are offered Monday 3 pm and 4.30 pm, Tuesday to Saturday 11.30 am, 3 pm and 4.30 pm, Sunday 11.30 am, 4 pm and 5 pm. The "La Fornace di Meleto" restaurant belongs to the winery. Bed & breakfast rooms are located on the first floor of the castle. Six apartments were created by restoring estate outhouses directly extended at the castle walls.

Recommended wines: Castello di Meleto Chianti Classico D.O.C.G., Castello di Meleto Chianti Classico Riserva D.O.C.G.

Chianti

Castello di Nipozzano
Marchesi de' Frescobaldi, 50060 Pelago, Italy
T +39 055 831 105 0, F +39 055 211 527
www.frescobaldi.it, adriane.riccato@frescobaldi.it

Open Monday 2 pm to 6.30 pm, Tuesday to Friday 10.30 am to 1 pm and 2 pm to 6.30 pm, Saturday and last Sunday in month 10.30 am to 1 pm (summer); Tuesday to Friday 10.30 am to 1 pm and 2 pm to 6.30 pm (winter). Castello di Nipozzano offers a wine shop. Guided cellar tours and tastings by appointment.

Recommended wines: Nipozzano Riserva Chianti Rùfina D.O.C.G., Montesodi Chianti Rùfina D.O.C.G., Mormoreto IGT

Chianti

Castello di Querceto
Via A. François 2, 50020 Greve in Chianti, Italy
T +39 055 859 21, F +39 055 859 2200
www.castellodiquerceto.it, querceto@castellodiquerceto.it

Open Monday to Friday 9 am to 5 pm, Saturday 2 pm to 6 pm (summer). Castello di Querceto offers a wine shop. Wine tasting by appointment (with guided cellar tour and typical Tuscan snack). The castle's gardens are open to the public. The living quarters are private. The estate has 10 apartments dedicated to farmhouse hospitality ("agriturismo").

Recommended wines: Il Pichio Chianti Classico Riserva D.O.C.G., La Corte IGT, Cignale IGT

Chianti

Fattoria Castello di Verrazzano
Via San Martino in Valle 12, Greti, 50022 Greve in Chianti, Italy
T +39 055 854 243, F +39 055 854 241
www.verrazzano.com, info@verrazzano.com

Open Monday to Friday 8 am to noon, and 1 pm to 5 pm. Wine shop and tastings. Thematic guided tours through the winery, historical cellars and gardens by appointment. A restaurant is available for wine tour participants. Guest accommodation is available at "Foresteria La Casanuova" approx. 0.6 miles (1 km) from the Castle. The Estate hosts the Verrazzano Center for Historical Studies.

Recommended wines: Castello di Verrazzano Chianti Classico D.O.C.G.

Montalcino

Altesino S.p.A.
Azienda Agricola, Località Altesino 54, 53024 Torrenieri di Montalcino, Italy
T +39 0577 806 208, F +39 0577 806 131
www.altesino.it, info@altesino.it

Open daily 9 am to 1 pm and 2 pm to 6.30 pm. Tastings and guided cellar tours by appointment.

Recommended wines: Altesino Brunello di Montalcino Riserva D.O.C.G., Altesino Brunello di Montalcino Riserva Montosoli D.O.C.G.

Montalcino

Castello Banfi
Località S. Angelo Scalo
53024 Montalcino, Italy
T +39 0577 840 111, F +39 0577 840 205
www.castellobanfi.com, info@castellobanfi.com

Open daily 10 am to 7 pm (April to October), 10 am to 6 pm (November to March). The wine shop is located at Castello Banfi, winery and cellars can be found 2.5 miles (4 km) south of the castle. Guided cellar tours are offered Monday to Friday by appointment. The "Taverna" restaurant and gourmet restaurant "Banfi" belong to the Castello. Luxurious guest rooms and suites are situated in the 18th Century hamlet and in the towers of the Castello. The Giovanni F. Mariani Glass Museum at Castello Banfi displays the world's most important collection of Roman glass goblets.

Recommended wines: Poggio all'Oro Brunello di Montalcino Riserva D.O.C.G., Poggio alle Mura Brunello di Montalcino Riserva D.O.C.G., SummuS Sant' Antimo D.O.C.

Montalcino

Ciacci Piccolomini d'Aragona
Località Molinello, 53024 Montalcino, Italy
T +39 0577 835 616, F +39 0577 835 785
www.ciaccipiccolomini.com, info@ciaccipiccolomini.com

Open Monday to Friday 9 am to 1 pm and 2 pm to 6 pm, on weekends by appointment only. Ciacci Piccolomini d'Aragona offers a wine shop. Tastings and guided tours by appointment. Small apartments are located in the center of Castelnuovo dell'Abate.

Recommended wines: Brunello di Montalcino D.O.C.G. Vigna di Pianrosso Riserva Santa Caterina d'Oro, FABIVS Sant' Antimo Rosso D.O.C.

South Africa

Cape Winelands

Vergelegen
Lourensford Road, Somerset West 7129, South Africa
T +27 (21) 847 1334, F +27 (21) 847 1608
www.vergelegen.co.za, winetasting@vergelegen.co.za

Open daily 9.30 am to 4.30 pm. Vergelegen has a wine tasting center. Guided cellar tours start at 10.30 am, 11.30 am and 3.30 pm. "Lady Phillips" restaurant offers lunch à la carte, the "Rose Terrace" provides al fresco lunches during summer months. Picnic facilities can be found in the Camphor-wood forest. The extensive gardens are open to the public.

Recommended wines: Vergelegen V, Vergelegen Red, Vergelegen White

Cape Winelands

Graham Beck Franschhoek Estate
PO Box 134, Franschhoek 7690, South Africa
T +27 21 874 1258, F +27 21 874 1712
www.grahambeckwines.co.za, market@grahambeckwines.co.za

Open Monday to Friday 9 am to 5 pm, Saturday 10 am to 4 pm. Possibility of tasting and buying wine. Guided tours by appointment. Sculptures and artwork are on display at the winery.

Recommended wines: Pheasants' Run, The Ridge Syrah, The Joshua

Cape Winelands

Nederburg Wines
Private Bag X 3006, Paarl 7620, South Africa
T +27 21 862 3104, F +27 21 862 4887
www.nederburg.co.za, nedwines@distell.co.za

Open Monday to Friday 8.30 am to 5 pm, Saturday 10 am to 2 pm. Extended hours from November to March: Saturday 10 am to 4 pm and Sunday 11 am to 4 pm. Possibility of tasting and buying wine directly at the winery. Guided tours Monday to Friday 10.30 am and 3 pm, Saturday 11 am. November to March also Sunday 11 am. Food and wine pairings and picnic lunches are served by appointment.

Recommended wines: Nederburg Classic, Nederburg Manor House

Photo Credits

Photographs by Christoph Kraneburg

except courtesy

Authors and Editors Christian Datz, Christof Kullmann

Layout a:dk publishing, Mainz

Photo Assistant Italy Michael Kopietz, Hamburg

Imaging ScanComp, Wiesbaden

Translations by SAW Communications
Dr. Sabine A. Werner, Mainz
English Conan Kirkpatrick
French Brigitte Villaumié
Spanish Carmen de Miguel
Italian Alessandra Carboni-Riehn

Editorial project by a:dk publishing, Mainz
www.adk-publishing.de

Published by teNeues Publishing Group

teNeues Verlag GmbH + Co. KG
Am Selder 37, 47906 Kempen, Germany
Tel.: 0049-(0)2152-916-0, Fax: 0049-(0)2152-916-111
E-mail: books@teneues.de

teNeues Publishing Company
16 West 22nd Street, New York, NY 10010, USA
Tel.: 001-212-627-9090, Fax: 001-212-627-9511

teNeues Publishing UK Ltd.
P.O. Box 402, West Byfleet, KT14 7ZF, Great Britain
Tel.: 0044-1932-403509, Fax: 0044-1932-403514

teNeues France S.A.R.L.
93, rue Bannier, 45000 Orléans, France
Tel.: 0033-2-38541071, Fax: 0033-1-38625340

Press department: arehn@teneues.de
Tel.: 0049-(0)2152-916-202

www.teneues.com

© 2007 teNeues Verlag GmbH + Co. KG, Kempen

ISBN: 978-3-8327-9145-2

Printed in Italy

Bibliographic information published by Die Deutsche Bibliothek. Die Deutsche Bibliothek lists this publication in the Deutsche Nationalbibliografie; detailed bibliographic data is available in the Internet at http://dnb.ddb.de.